Attending upon God without Distraction

Attending upon God without Distraction

by

Nathanael Vincent

Introduced by Joel R. Beeke
Edited by Don Kistler

Soli Deo Gloria Publications
An imprint of Reformation Heritage Books
Grand Rapids, Michigan

Attending upon God without Distraction
© 2010 by Reformation Heritage Books

Soli Deo Gloria Publications
An imprint of Reformation Heritage Books
3070 29th St. SE
Grand Rapids, MI 49512
616-977-0889
orders@heritagebooks.org
www.heritagebooks.org

This book was originally published in London in 1695 under the title *The Cure of Distractions in Attending upon God.* This Soli Deo Gloria reprint has undergone spelling, grammatical, and formatting changes. All rights reserved. Printed in the USA.

Paperback reprint 2023

ISBN 979-8-88686-023-8

The Library of Congress has cataloged the hardcover edition as follows:

Vincent, Nathanael, 1639?-1697.
 [Cure of distractions in attending upon God]
  Attending upon God without distraction / by Nathanael Vincent ; introduction by Joel R. Beeke ; edited by Don Kistler.
   p. cm.
  Originally published: The cure of distractions in attending upon God. London, 1695. With spelling, grammatical, and formatting changes.
  ISBN 978-1-60178-093-5 (hardcover : alk. paper) 1. Spiritual life–Puritans. 2. Attention–Religious aspects–Puritans. I. Kistler, Don. II. Title.
 BV4501.3.V56 2010
 248.4'858–dc22
                    2010017587

For additional Reformed literature, both new and used, request a free book list from Reformation Heritage Books at the above address.

Contents

Biographical Introduction. vii
The Epistle Dedicatory ix
To the Reader. xiii

PART ONE
Everyone Ought to Attend upon God

1. What Attending upon God Is 3
2. What Attending upon God Implies 16
3. Various Kinds of Attending upon God. 26
4. Why We Ought to Attend upon God 39
5. Reproofs for Those Who Reject
   Attending upon God. 47
6. Exhortations for Those Who Reject
   Attending upon God 54
7. Directions and Consolations for Attending
   upon God. 63

PART TWO
*Attending upon God Means We Should
Look upon Him as Lord and Serve Him*

8. How God Is the Lord. 79
9. How God's Lordship Should Impact Our
   Attending upon Him 92
10. Reproofs and Advice for Those Who Don't
    Attend upon God as Lord 100

PART THREE
Attending upon God Should Be without Distraction

11. How the Heart Is Distracted 109
12. How to Attend upon God without Distraction. 121
13. The Evils of Distractions and Benefits
    of Avoiding Them 128

PART FOUR
*Cases of Conscience and Applications of
Attending upon God without Distractions*

14. Cases of Conscience about Distractions 143
15. Cautions and Expostulations about Distractions. ... 158
16. Directions to Remedies against Distractions 175
17. Advice for Avoiding Distractions in
    Religious Duties 185
18. Terrors of Distractions and Encouragements
    to Believers 199

BIOGRAPHICAL INTRODUCTION

Nathanael Vincent
(ca. 1639–1697)

Nathanael Vincent was born in Cornwall to John Vincent, a non-conformist minister, and his wife, Sarah. He was the younger brother of Thomas. A brilliant child, Nathanael memorized and repeated sermons at age seven. He graduated from Christ Church, Oxford, with a Bachelor of Arts degree in 1656 and a Master of Arts in 1657. He was then appointed chaplain of the Corpus Christi College.

Vincent was ordained at age twenty-one and became rector of Langley Marish, Buckinghamshire. Ejected by the Act of Uniformity of 1662, he spent three years as a private chaplain to Sir Henry Blount and his wife, Hester, at Tittenhanger, Hertfordshire, before moving to London in 1666. A large meetinghouse was built in Farthing Alley, Southwark, to accommodate the crowds that came to hear him preach. That drew the attention of the authorities, who began to harass him. On one occasion, soldiers with muskets surrounded his pulpit. When Vincent refused to stop preaching, the soldiers pulled him out of the pulpit by his hair and dragged him through the streets. He was fined and sent to prison. After several months of imprisonment, he was sentenced to banishment from the country, but a flaw in the indictment prevented that sentence from being carried out.

In 1672, Vincent was licensed as a Presbyterian preacher. It was not long, however, before he was persecuted again for preaching. On one occasion in 1681, his meetinghouse was visited by "three justices with constables and other officers." Vincent continued to preach even though the uproar of the audience became so great that he could scarcely be heard. When the justices then commanded the people to disperse, the whole congregation broke out into singing, during which time Vincent managed to escape through a side exit. Two years later, Vincent was charged for conventicling and sentenced to a three-month prison term. Four years later, he was arrested and falsely accused of taking part in Monmouth's Rebellion.

Vincent's imprisonments left him so weak that for some time he was unable to preach, and resorted to writing. Most of his fourteen books were written in prison. His books reflect a warm, experiential piety expressed according to the Ramistic method of outlining. His love and concern for the body of Christ is evident in every book.

Attending upon God without Distraction invites and exhorts us to a close life with God through Christ, and shows us how to attend upon God as our Savior and Lord. Various cases of conscience, cautions, directions, and challenges are addressed with biblical and practical winsomeness and forcefulness. In some ways, this book seems even more applicable in our hurried and harried day than in Nathanael Vincent's own day. Though the content remains unaltered, I have taken the liberty to divide this treatise into four parts and considerably smaller chapters. Our hearty thanks to Don Kislter for his initial editing work.

Vincent died suddenly in 1697, at age fifty-eight; he was survived by his wife, Anna, and six children. His funeral was conducted by Nathaniel Taylor. He was buried in the nonconformists' burial ground at Bunhill Fields.

The Epistle Dedicatory

To the Truly Honorable Sir William Ashurst, Knight, and Alderman of the City of London

Much Honored Sir,

    I did not address you when you were like the rising sun, and made the chief seat in this city, where you were deservedly placed to shine with more than ordinary luster; when you discovered and were severe against the works of darkness, and your influence was so benign and kind for the sustenance and benefit of London. But now you have run your course so well, and have done so without the least cloud; nay, with so much clearness and glory. I make this dedication to you, desiring your serious perusal of a treatise, the subject of which is of such great importance. And indeed now that you have quit the chair and have less public business to manage, and may have more leisure to retire into yourself, and from company and from civil affairs; this *Cure of Distractions* in religious duties knocks at your door, the author desiring that it may be helpful to your meditations and devotion.

    'Tis a great respect and honor that is due to the gods on earth, as magistrates are called, and inferiors should apply to them accordingly, with a great sense of their distance. With what reverence then are we to approach the supreme Majesty, the Lord of Hosts, the King of glory! Our highest apprehensions are infinitely below Him, and the best of saints would rather worship Him than perform anything that is unworthy of the name of worship.

Among the many faults in holy duties, there is one that will never be quite mended in this world, and that is distraction; but yet more and more help may be still attained against it. And these sermons with which I now present you, I hope may, with a blessing from heaven, contribute something and be successful in this way.

If religious duties were but well done, everything else would be done the better; for it is from God alone that we have ability to do as we ought in any matter whatsoever. The Lord gives wisdom and grace most liberally to them who most sincerely seek Him. And such as have most help from God will best perform their duty towards man; and both church and state will find them the most useful members. Religion is certainly the truest policy. The wisdom of this world, says the apostle, and of the princes of this world, comes to naught; but the power of godliness makes men better in every capacity and relation. How it alters and amends persons, families, and nations where it is encouraged and prevails! Righteousness and peace, joy and love, are found to be the blessed effects of true religion. It tames the fierceness and subdues the malignity of corrupt nature, and makes man to look something like what he was in the state of innocence.

All who wish well to this city and nation must desire that God may be better served, and that men by His service may be bettered. How happy would we be if people were all righteous! Violence then would be no more heard in our land, nor wasting and destruction within our borders; our walls would be called salvation, and our gates praise, and the Lord Himself would be to us an everlasting Light, and our God our glory!

I wish that all lord mayors for the future may follow your example, and endeavor to suppress wickedness, and that they may never be ashamed of holiness, which is the glory of God, and is most unreasonably looked upon as matter of disgrace to any man. Sir, you are descended from religious ancestors, and religion is that which truly ennobles your blood and family. An increase of this nobility and of all other blessings is wished to yourself and yours, Honored Sir, by your most humble servant,

—Nathanael Vincent

To the Reader

Reader, it is a subject of the highest consequence, and in which all are concerned, that I address in this treatise. I design some relief against that which is the general complaint of serious Christians, who would fain offer to God more spiritual and well-pleasing sacrifices, but are hindered by the remaining sin and vanity of their own minds. They are called indeed the habitations of God through the Spirit; but these habitations are haunted with distracting thoughts and vain imaginations, to their great grief and disturbance. The work and service of the God of heaven is the principal business everyone has to do in this world; and though no duties are to be slightly done to man which are done for the Lord's sake, yet, in attendance upon Himself, and in those duties which more immediately we perform to Him, a holy awe becomes us. Our hearts should be immovably fixed, and we should exert the utmost vigor of our spirits. To trifle with a jealous God, whose all-seeing eye strictly observes all we do, and wherever we fail, is to despise Him to His face, and to act to the great peril of our own souls.

"Our God," said the apostle, "is a consuming fire." And Nadab and Abihu, the sons of Aaron, found Him so to their cost and sorrow when they "offered strange fire, such as he commanded them not." We must do what God commands, and as He commands, else what we call our religious duties will be looked upon by Him as acts of disobedience.

Ever since the first man parted from God, the mind of man is notoriously fickle and wavering. Being unsettled by sin, it roves up and down the earth from one vanity to another; but with what difficulty is it brought back to God! And though it is engaged to approach near to Him, yet if it is not narrowly watched, in the twinkling of an eye it starts back and is gone away from Him. To keep our hearts with all diligence is our duty, but they will not be held in from wandering by our most careful custody. It is the hand of that God alone, by which the whole universe consists and is kept from dissolution, that can fix the mind of man and hinder its being distracted in His service.

A great deal of pain is taken in the world to little purpose. "All things," said Solomon, "are full of labor; man cannot utter it." And yet he affirms that there is no profit under the sun. But it is lamentable to think that in the church there should be so much labor in vain. Distraction of mind keeps the heart away from God, and from the duty that seems to be performed to Him; it hinders the stirring of holy affections and the actions of saving grace, and it turns religion into a mere bodily exercise. And how can that be profitable to the soul which is a great way off, and so little regards what is done? How can it be acceptable to God, who is a Spirit, and will be worshipped in Spirit and in truth?

The Church of Rome is for implicit faith, for blind obedience, and for worship in an unknown tongue. How distracted must that worship be? How can the people's thoughts be intent upon what they do not understand? Too many Protestants in their devotions mind what they themselves say as little as if they did not understand the words they spoke. And truly the Protestants sin with greater aggravation because, though they have means of better instruction, their duties are no better performed.

The cure of distraction in religious services is very difficult. Some think lightly of the disease and imagine the cure needless; others are discouraged from striving against distractions, as if it were impossible to overcome them—but nothing is too hard for the great Physician. He can heal the mind's vanity and bring the heart into God's presence; He is able to cast down imaginations, to hinder them from rising again, and to bring thoughts into captivity and obedience.

A sense of my own wanderings in those ordinances I administer and engage in has put me upon a more serious study how to prevent them. And I would be the first and best follower myself of that counsel which I give to others. And if the Lord is served with greater attention and spirituality, and if the hearts of those who shall read this treatise are more than ever in the work of God, and more benefited by doing it, the great end is obtained, which is designed by

—Nathanael Vincent

PART ONE

Everyone Ought to Attend upon God

CHAPTER 1

What Attending upon God Is

> "That ye may attend upon the Lord
> without distraction."
> —1 Corinthians 7:35

The Apostle Paul had a great and fervent zeal for the honor of God, that He might have such attendance as He commands, and which most rightfully appertains to a Lord so great and good. Unto Him both heaven and earth owe all service and obedience. The apostle also manifests an extraordinary care for the souls of men, that they might not fail to give that attendance which is enjoined them as their duty, and which is also their advantage, honor, and security. The thoughts, the hearts, and the endeavors of all should run in this way as to a matter of the mightiest importance and concern. Here, if we are undistractedly serious and sincere, all is safe—and that both throughout time and to eternity. But if attendance upon God is either neglected or negligently given, though we are never so intent and industrious about other things, our souls and all our labor will be lost together.

In 1 Corinthians 7, a little before our text, the apostle admonishes the Corinthian saints of the shortness of time and of the transitoriness of this present world, and then informs them what kind of attendance upon Himself God requires and expects from them.

His admonition concerning time is startling in verse 29: "the time is short." The allusion here is to sails that are no longer spread, but are bound up when the ship is just come to the harbor. The word also signifies to wind up a body in grave clothes so that it may be fit for the sepulcher. Time is thus ready to be wound up continually, and to be buried, as it were, in eternity, compared to which it is but as a drop to the whole ocean, and this very drop is ever wasting. Time is a short thing, in a continual flux, and every moment growing shorter. Other things are of less value because they can be enjoyed but for a little while; the epithet "temporal," or lasting only "for a season," when added to the greatest wealth—the highest pleasures, nay, even to diadems and kingdoms—makes them fall in the esteem of a discerning judgment. But the worth of time is enhanced by the brevity of it. The day of salvation, the acceptable time in which we, and our attendance upon God, may be accepted, cannot extend beyond the limits of the time of life. Now we must make peace with God, work out our own salvation, and provide for eternity; this must be done now or never. There is not a moment of time but is too good to be lost; there is service and work enough to do in it, and to lose all our time is to everlastingly lose ourselves.

The apostle speaks of the world's transitoriness: the "fashion of the world passes away." Mammon is but a sorry master, and really is unworthy of that frequent attendance and mighty respect that is given to it. Sin has made man foolish and the world vain. And it is an undeniable argument of man's folly that a vain world is so concerned over those things that are so apt to fade and change.

As scenes in a comedy or tragedy alternate, and quickly the last act comes, and the play is at an end, so this world is continually varying. Now there appears one, and a little after quite another face of things. The face of the sky is not more mutable than the state of human affairs. And thus it is likely to be until the world's end, when "the earth also and the works that are therein shall be burned up" (2 Peter 3:10).

That God whom Christians attend upon is unchangeable, and so is His love for them; and the inheritance they expect hereafter is "incorruptible, and fadeth not away." But they themselves are strangers and pilgrims in this world, and should behave themselves as passengers who are traveling toward a better world. And as for their enjoyments by the way, they should love them as if they were about to leave them. Joy should be moderate in the fruition of them; and when they are taken away, sorrow should not be excessive, nor transgress the bounds of grace and reason.

The apostle, as a man well acquainted with the court of heaven, directs believers' attendance upon the Lord, who dwells and reigns there. He is very careful not to cast a snare upon the Corinthians, nor to impose upon conscience what God does not impose. Papal authority is audacious and antichristian, and is bold to command (and that upon the highest penalty) what the Lord never required. But the apostle abhors spiritual usurpation. He would have all observe what God called them to, and in every condition to abide with God, and to "attend upon the Lord without distraction."

In these words take notice of the Lord with whom we have to do. The eyes of servants are to their masters and the eyes of worshippers should be to the Lord whom they adore. And if they had a greater respect for this Holy One, what an influence it would have upon their lives and services! The word *Kurio*, or "Lord" in the New Testament, is put for "Jehovah" in the Old. The God whom Christians acknowledge is the Lord Jehovah, who has His being of Himself, has dominion over all.

Observe what this Lord requires and calls for, and that is attendance upon Him. The Greek word which the Holy Ghost uses is very significant and emphatic. It implies access unto God and abiding with Him, and being fit for and well pleased with both.

Who is to attend upon the Lord? All men owe homage and service to Him, which is their honor and interest to pay. But those who are His own children and people are by special obligations and favor called to this duty and privilege of attending upon their God, and they have a new principle and nature that inclines them to it.

Here is a direction as to the manner of attending on the Lord: it must be without distraction. Plutarch says that the study of wisdom occurs without distraction when nothing is able to call away the mind and make it cease that study. In attending upon God, there must be intention in the mind and a full bent of the heart, with strength of affection and desire, not to be diverted, much less extinguished. All other business, comparatively, must be looked upon as trivial; attendance upon the Lord must be with the greatest seriousness.

I derive three doctrines from the words:

First, the children of men ought to attend upon God; this the text plainly supposes.

Second, in attending upon God we should look upon Him as the Lord and serve Him accordingly.

Third, attendance upon the Lord should be without distraction.

DOCTRINE 1. The children of men ought to attend upon God. The heaven of heavens is His throne, and He is attended on by thousands and ten thousands of glorious and holy ones who minister unto Him and stand before Him. And yet upon earth, which is His footstool, He calls for attendance too; for

He "rejoices in the habitable parts of the earth, and his delights are with the sons of men," who understand Him and themselves so well as to seek after Him. He requires continually to be waited on. Hosea 12:6: "Therefore turn thou to thy God: keep mercy and judgment, and wait on thy God continually." Injunctions to wait are reiterated, with the encouraging promise of divine aid and strengthening grace. Psalm 27:14: "Wait on the LORD: be of good courage, and he shall strengthen thy heart: wait, I say, on the LORD." Psalm 37:34: "Wait on the LORD, and keep his way." This way is true; walking in it is holy and safe, and its end is peace.

In handling this doctrine I shall, first, show you what is supposed in man's attendance upon God; second, tell you what is implied in this attendance; third, speak of several sorts of attending upon the Lord; fourth, assign the reasons why the children of men ought to give their attendance upon God; and, fifth, make application.

First, I am to show you what is supposed in man's attendance upon God. There are several prerequisites for this; for man is not easily persuaded to this duty, though the performance of it proves never so beneficial to him. Now, that there may be this attendance:

1. Man must firmly believe that there is a God. Hebrews 11:6: "But without faith it is impossible to please him; for he that cometh to God must believe that he is." As God is *to* everlasting, so He is *from* everlasting. If He had not ever been, and that of Himself, he would never have been; neither could anything else ever have had a being. The existence of creatures supposes that there is a Creator, and attendance upon God supposes that there is a God to be attended on. The stronger the assent to this truth is, the greater will be the care to understand how the attendance may be acceptable. The being of a God, few

will deny in words; but there is an abundance who deny Him in their works, even among those who profess to know Him. And being so foolish as to say in their hearts that there is no God, it is no wonder that with their hearts they refuse to seek Him.

Man should look upward and see how the heavens declare the glory of God, and how the firmament shows His handiwork. The visible creation is not more obvious to the eye than the eternal power and Godhead of Him who made all things are clearly to be seen by the mind of man (Romans 1:20). And if man will but look into his own heart, he may find this truth deeply engraved there, that God is. Therefore the apostle speaks thus of the Gentiles, who had only the light of nature in Romans 1:19: "Because that which may be known of God is manifest in them; for God hath shewed it unto them." Let none go about to obliterate this truth concerning the being of a God, but undoubtingly accept it; for it is the first stone in the foundation of all truly religious service and obedience.

2. **Man must have a sense that he had his being from God and was made for Him**; and truly he is made such a creature that he will never be quite unmade so as to become nothing. He is capable of knowing and serving his Master, and enjoying Him forever. God has made all men for Himself, and in some way or another He will secure His own honor and have glory from the very worst. But as for His own people, He has formed, bought, and newly made them for Himself, that they might show forth His praise (Isaiah 43:21). Man should eye the hand that made him, and the end for which he was made. Our bodies will be found to be a curious piece of divine workmanship, if the construction, variety, and use of their parts are considered. But though our flesh is of God's forming, yet, in a more immediate manner, He is called the Father of our spirits. And wherefore have our souls a thinking faculty but that God may be thought

of? Why do we have memories but that our Creator from our youth may be remembered? And if we live to have gray hairs, He in no wise is to be forgotten. Why are we capable of loving, desiring, and taking delight but that God may be the chief Object of these affections? In Him we live, and move, and have our being (Acts 17:28), so that we might live to Him, move according to His will, and be indeed His servants.

3. Man must be persuaded that God is rightfully his Ruler, and has given him a law and commandments by which he is to be governed. Mammon and Satan are mere usurpers, and where they reign they ruin. The evil one is to be resisted, not obeyed; and man was made to have dominion over the creatures, not to be enslaved by them. But God is man's Sovereign by right, and may lay upon man what commands He pleases; and yet He has given them none but what are holy, just, and good (Romans 7:12). And the better these are obeyed, man becomes more holy, just, and good himself, and partakes more of the divine nature. Would we attend upon God? We must have respect unto His commands. David plainly intimates the gain of obedience when he says, "More are they to be esteemed than gold, yea, than much fine gold." He signifies the pleasure of obedience when he adds, "sweeter also than honey and the honeycomb" (Psalm 19:10).

4. Man must be convinced that by sin he has departed from God, and has justly incurred His displeasure. The natural distance between God and man as a creature must ever remain. God is, and will be forever, infinitely above and superior even to those who are in heaven. He "humbleth himself to behold the things that are in heaven" (Psalm 113:6). But the moral distance that is between God and man, or the enmity that sin is the cause of, may be eliminated. When man attends upon God, he should come with a deep sense of how he has provoked

Him, that he is by nature a child of wrath (Ephesians 2:3), and in his practice a rebel. And since man has acted like an enemy, so he deserves to be dealt with as one.

When the Syrians came to the king of Israel, they had sackcloth on their loins and ropes on their heads (1 Kings 20:32). They had newly been in arms against him, and now they declare how ill they deserve to be treated by him. For offenders to approach God without any trouble for their offenses is not to attend upon Him, but to affront Him. These are His own words: "Woe to them! for they have fled from me: destruction unto them! because they have transgressed against me" (Hosea 7:13). And hear the language of the penitent church in Lamentations 5:16: "The crown is fallen from our head; woe to us, that we have sinned!" When we come for mercy, we must be sensible that mercy is undeserved and that "to us belongeth confusion of face" (Daniel 9:8). There should be a penitential acknowledgment that we have been foolish, disobedient, and deceived; that we have served various lusts and pleasures, and in ourselves are so hateful to God that we are unworthy to be admitted into the number of His attendants.

5. Man must hear the call of God to return to Him, and to obedience and duty. The angels who sinned were not spared, nor called to attend upon God in order to gain recovery after their apostasy. Indeed, we find Satan an intruder among "the sons of God," who "came to present themselves before the LORD" (Job 1:6), but it was not to beg grace for himself; his chains of darkness hindered his hope of finding any. He comes as an accuser of Job, and desiring permission to do him mischief. But man, though departed from God, is called to come back again. Hosea 14:1: "O Israel, return unto the LORD thy God; for thou hast fallen by thine iniquity." Man is sought after as well as saved, or sought that he may be saved. And if the

Lord did not seek him, but left him to his own imagination and inclination, his imaginations are so vain, his inclinations so perverse and wicked, that he would never cease going astray till he died without wisdom. The call of God is loud and earnest, that man would turn from his disobedience and do his duty. Proverbs 8:4: "Unto you, O men, I call; and my voice is to the sons of man." Proverbs 1:23: "Turn you at my reproof: behold, I will pour out my spirit unto you, I will make known my words unto you." Proverbs 8:34: "Blessed is the man that heareth me, watching daily at my gates, waiting at the posts of my doors."

6. Man must look upon God as accessible in Christ. When Adam fell into the first transgression, showing a contempt of God and of His covenant, and the life that was there promised, he was turned out of Paradise, and a flaming sword was placed to hinder his reentering and gaining access to the tree of life. Life could no longer be had by the first covenant; therefore he and his faith were directed to the promised seed, who would bruise the serpent's head. And in time He would be manifested to destroy the works of the devil (1 John 3:8). This work of the devil was sin, whereby man had departed from his Maker. Now Christ, the second Adam, suffered once for sins, the Just for the unjust, that He might bring man to God, and make up the breach that sin had made between them (1 Peter 3:18). As God is but One, so there is but one Mediator between God and men, the man Christ Jesus, who gave Himself a ransom for all (1 Timothy 2:5–6), and there is no access to God by any other. But, says the apostle, "in Christ Jesus our Lord…we have boldness and access with confidence by the faith of him" (Ephesians 3:11–12). Under the Old Testament there was but one temple, one altar for burnt offering and sin offering to make an atonement. A heathen thought it a dishonor to the Lord Jehovah that Hezekiah had taken away His high places and His altars,

and had commanded Judah and Jerusalem to worship before one altar (2 Chronicles 32:12). But the mystery and meaning of this was that Jesus Christ alone is the Way, the Truth, and the Life, and that no man comes to the Father but by Him.

7. Man must plainly discern his ignorance and impotence to give a right attendance upon God, without the direction and aid of His Word and Spirit. Nay, as man lacks both skill and strength to serve the Lord, so he has no will to do it; there is an indisposition and even an ill disposition in him, which plainly shows that the light and grace of the Word and Spirit are of absolute necessity for an attendance upon God that is acceptable to Him. When man goes off from God and takes himself to himself in matters of religion, he ranges infinitely, like a seafaring man who has lost his compass in a mist, moving swiftly, but to no purpose. Then there shall be more words than what is written, more articles than what God has put into our creed, more commands than the Lawgiver ever gave; nay, more gods and more mediators than one. Man's invention will be fruitlessly fruitful, and himself restless and endless in his own ways. We should see our need of instruction and help from the Spirit of the Lord. Both light and liberty, strength and liveliness in all holy duties are from Him.

It is through the Son as Mediator, and it is by the Spirit as our Helper, that we have access to the Father (Ephesians 2:18). The apostle acknowledges in Romans 8:26, "the Spirit also helpeth our infirmities: for we know not what we should pray for as we ought." The holy and gracious desires of the saints are the breathings of this Spirit in them; acceptable petitions that will find audience are of His drawing up and editing. "He maketh intercession for the saints according to the will of God" (Romans 8:27). He is the Instructor of all those who are taught to profit. Ordinances, gifts, and administrations, which are so useful, are from the Spirit, and the benefit and success of them is owing to Him. His aid is earnestly to be implored and thankfully to be accepted. Preparation for attendance upon God is necessary. Psalm 10:17: "Thou wilt prepare their heart, thou wilt cause thine ear to hear." And this preparation is the work of the Spirit.

8. Man must not doubt, but must be thoroughly persuaded that God is ready to be found of such as attend upon Him, and is a rewarder of them who diligently seek Him (Hebrews 11:6). Satan pretends to be the representer of God to man, and he represents Him in two contrary ways. Both ways are false, and are indeed misrepresentations. From secure souls, he endeavors to hide the wrath of God, His holiness, justice, and jealousy, so that he may heighten presumption. From awakened and humble hearts, he endeavors to conceal His mercy and grace in Christ so that he may kill their hope and discourage them from engaging in the work of God. But 'tis wisdom in man to hear what the Lord speaks of Himself; for He best knows Himself, and the revelations He makes of Himself are most certainly true. Now as He has told us that He would wound the head of His enemies, and as He accounts those His enemies who go on still in their trespasses (Psalm 68:21), so He has assured us that He is good and ready to forgive those who are troubled because they have offended, and who see their need of pardon. He is "plenteous in mercy unto all them that call upon" Him (Psalm 86:5).

It is a mighty encouragement to attend upon God when we see the door of hope standing open, and that the Lord takes pleasure in those who fear His displeasure and hope in His mercy (Psalm 147:11). The tables of the Law were put into the ark, and the mercy seat was above it, a plain intimation that the Lord who sits upon this mercy seat will not enter into judgment with His servants nor mark their iniquities, but will be merciful to the unrighteousness of them who turn to Him. This should raise hope in dejected spirits, and cause that hope to abound. Psalm 130:7–8: "Let Israel hope in the LORD: for with the LORD there is mercy, and with him is plenteous redemption. And he shall redeem Israel from all his iniquities."

9. Man must not think to divide his service between God and mammon. Our Lord Himself tells us that "No man can serve two masters; for either he will hate the one and love the other, or else he will hold to the one, and despise the other. Ye cannot serve God and mammon." To mind the world as if it were the most desirable thing, and to serve the Lord only for the world's sake, is hateful earthly mindedness and hypocrisy. When the children of Israel assembled themselves before God only for corn and wine, their cries were but howlings in His ears (Hosea 7:14). If we would attend upon God, we must come out from the world. Conformity to the world and walking after the course of it must cease. The most desirable good things of it must be condemned in comparison with God and the better and enduring substance. We shall never look and aim so as to obtain the things that are unseen and eternal unless the eye is shut against the things that are seen and temporal (2 Corinthians 4:18).

Attenders upon God may and ought to mind their secular business which their particular callings lead them to. Christians are cautioned against idleness as great disorderliness, and are commanded and exhorted by our Lord Jesus Christ "with quietness to work, and to eat their own bread" (2 Thessalonians 3:12). This, notwithstanding, must ever be remembered: that the things of this world are to be regarded so far as God has commanded, that they must be begged of Him, and kept, used, and improved for Him. They must not be liked for themselves, but so far as God is enjoyed with them and in them. And in the greatest abundance of them, this should be the heart's language, which came from the heart and mouth of Luther: "Lord, I will not be put off with such things as these! 'The Lord is my portion,' saith my soul; and I have looked and longed and wait for Thy salvation!"

10. Man must consent to cast away whatever may come between the Lord and him. And what that is, the prophet plainly tells us in Isaiah 59:1–2: "Behold, the Lord's hand is not shortened that it cannot save, neither his ear heavy that it cannot hear; but your iniquities have separated between you and your God, and your sins have hid his face from you, that he will not hear." Separation from God is the hell of hell; and this hell upon earth is caused by sin. Sin is that which provokes the Lord to be angry with man, and with His soul to hate him; to behold him afar off so that he is not admitted into His favor, or unto fellowship and communion with Him. To talk of fellowship with God and to walk in this darkness of sin is to lie to others and to deceive ourselves. This middle wall of partition must be thrown down, or else there can be no drawing nigh unto God. James 4:8: "Draw nigh to God, and he will draw nigh to you. Cleanse your hands, ye sinners; purify your hearts, ye double-minded." The hand must not practice and work wickedness; the heart must not regard and like it. The more the heart is desirous of purity, the more fit it is to attend upon the Lord, to serve Him and to see Him. Therefore you read in Matthew 5:8, "Blessed are the pure in heart, for they shall see God." And 2 Corinthians 6:17–18: "Wherefore come out from among them, and be ye separate, saith the Lord, and touch not the unclean thing; and I will receive you, and will be a Father unto you, and ye shall be my sons and daughters, saith the Lord Almighty."

CHAPTER 2

What Attending upon God Implies

Second, I am to tell you what is implied in man's attendance upon God. This attendance has many components and takes in all the service He commands. In Scripture it is expressed sometimes by following God, sometimes by waiting upon the Lord, and in our text by attending on Him. I shall explain what this attending on God is in several particulars:

1. Attending upon God implies inquiring of God. He is "only wise," says Paul (Romans 16:27), the "Father of Lights," from whom all true wisdom and every good and perfect gift come down (James 1:17). The wisdom of this world, and of the princes of this world, however it is magnified as the most profound policy, cannot secure them who are most blessed with it; but they and their wisdom come to nought and perish together. But spiritual wisdom, which is hidden from the prudent of the world and is the special gift of God, is ordained to the glory of them who have it (1 Corinthians 2:6–7). Wisdom that brings salvation and everlasting glory deserves the name of wisdom. Sound wisdom, it may well be called, as in Proverbs 2:6–7: "For the Lord giveth wisdom: out of his mouth cometh knowledge and understanding. He layeth up sound wisdom for the righteous: he is a buckler to them that walk uprightly."

We must inquire of God for wisdom of this nature. He gives it to all who desire and ask for it, and that liberally without upbraiding (James 1:5). He does not upbraid any with their former hatred of knowledge or contempt of wisdom; neither does He upbraid them with their natural dullness and inaptness to learn — but both instruction and the very heart and ability to receive it are from Him. Proverbs 20:12: "The hearing ear, and the seeing eye, the LORD hath made even both of them." The psalmist thus desired to attend upon God all the days of his life that he might inquire in His temple (Psalm 27:4). They are well counseled, and are led safely to glory, who have God to be their guide even unto death, and still follow on to know the Lord.

2. Attending upon God implies hearkening to and heeding what God speaks. Psalm 85:8: "I will hear what God the LORD will speak." And what attention does such a Speaker deserve who speaks from heaven and whose Word shows the way to heaven, who speaks peace and publishes glad tidings of great salvation! When Lydia's heart was opened, she "attended unto those things which were spoken by Paul" (Acts 16:14). She heard Paul's voice, but believed the Lord spoke by him to her, and she regarded the message accordingly.

We attend upon God in the ministry of the Word when our eye looks beyond the minister unto the Lord Himself, and when our ear is attentive that we may understand His truths which are to be believed and His precepts that are to be obeyed. Now the Word comes with a divine power and efficacy when God is heard speaking in that Word. 1 Thessalonians 2:13: "For this cause also thank we God without ceasing, because, when ye received the word of God which ye heard of us, ye received it not as the word of men, but as it is in truth, the word of God, which effectually worketh also in you that believe." It concerns us to take heed what we hear, and how. We should be forward to be made acquainted with God's truth and will. And neither of these should be held in unrighteousness; for to hear what God speaks and not to mind it, but to act quite contrary, is disobedience with a high aggravation.

3. Attending upon God implies returning and yielding ourselves unto God. Man is naturally contentious and struggles hard about this point; he will not yield to God to direct and rule him. Rather, man thinks that it is reasonable that in all things God should submit and obey. Till man is instructed and enlightened from above, he will always be murmuring and disputing against his duty, and will not come to God, though God is light and can shine into his mind; though divine goodness can satiate man's soul; though the Lord has supreme and sufficient authority to command the conscience, and to lay the whole man under obligation to obedience. But when we attend upon God indeed, we hearken to His call to return, and we return at His call.

There cannot be a right attendance without sincere conversion, and this conversion is man's yielding of himself to his Lord. Romans 6:12–13: "Let not sin reign in your mortal bodies, that ye should obey it in the lusts thereof; neither yield ye your members as instruments of unrighteousness unto sin, but yield yourselves unto God, as those that are alive from the dead, and your members as instruments of righteousness unto God." The body must be yielded so that the Holy Ghost may consecrate it to the Lord's service; so that eyes and mouth, hands and feet, and all may be at God's beck and call, and ready to fulfill His pleasure. Especially must the heart be yielded, nay, the whole heart, else returning is but feigned. Jeremiah 3:10: "Her treacherous sister Judah hath not turned unto me with her whole heart, but feignedly, saith the LORD." The soul must consent to have all its powers renewed and sanctified, that with them all it may give attendance upon God; the heart without any reservation must yield so that God should work out of it whatever is offensive, and that He should work in it that which is pleasing in His sight.

4. Attending upon God implies seeking and desiring after God. Isaiah 26:9: "With my soul have I desired thee in the night; yea, with my spirit within me will I seek thee early." The bent of the very soul was toward God, and the desires are kept up in vehemence both night and day. The Lord humbles Himself to behold things done in heaven, yet He looks down upon the children of men upon earth to see if there are any who understand and seek Him. And if He seeks after these seekers, how ready is He to be found by them! The command is that we should "seek the LORD, and his strength: seek his face evermore" (Psalm 105:4). God is to be sought after for Himself. When the all-sufficient Jehovah gives Himself to any, He gives infinitely more than if He gave them many thousand such worlds as this one is. His strength is of absolute necessity to secure us from evil and to assist us in doing good, and the shining of His face upon us makes our work easy and pleasant; it makes our life, and even death itself, comfortable. No wonder, therefore, when God said, "Seek ye my face," that one of His attendants heard presently, as the echo answers the voice, and said, "Thy face, LORD, will I seek" (Psalm 27:8). To seek anyone else is vain; it is seeking for water in a broken cistern that can hold none. Men of low degree, though never so great a multitude, are vanity; and men of highest degree are a lie (Psalm 62:9). But God's power, mercy, and truth are an evident proof that He is forward and sufficient to satiate the souls of all who charge their souls to wait only upon Him, and to have their expectations from Him.

5. Attending upon God implies waiting upon Him in His own house and sanctuary. Every Christian's house should be a house of prayer, but the place of public assembling to worship should be highly prized, and frequented for the sake of the work that is performed there. The living, the true, the eternal God is here publicly owned and acknowledged, and so is the only Mediator, Jesus, as well as the Holy Ghost, whose aid and grace are all in all, as to the efficacy and success of those ordinances which are administered. It is no marvel that saints who have seen God's power and glory in His sanctuary thirst for God, for the living God. And that is the language of their hearts: "When shall I come and appear before God?" (Psalm 42:2). As the sanctuary was next to the holiest of all, so the house of God on earth is, as it were, the suburbs of the city of God in heaven. The sanctuary is the place where the light of holy and heavenly doctrine shines. Here the psalmist understood the end of the ungodly, and that all their prosperity was but a dream and image, being abused by themselves to further and hasten their destruction; for they are quickly cast down from their greatest height and brought into desolation as in a moment, and utterly consumed with terrors (Psalm 73:17–19). Here also he understood how good God is to the Israelites even when He afflicts them. His rod guides them and purges their hearts. He upholds them with one hand while He corrects them with another. He makes earthly things more contemptible in their eyes and sets their affections more upon Himself, who is their Portion forever.

In the sanctuary believers are quickened, strengthened, comforted, and settled. And this one thing they desire of the Lord, and that they seek after, that they may dwell in the house of the Lord all the days of their life that they may behold the beauty of the Lord, His holiness and grace in Christ, with the admirable harmony of all His attributes; that they may perpetually be inquiring in His temple until, being guided unto death and brought safe to glory, they are past all danger (Psalm 27:4).

6. Attending upon God implies not only keeping the way of His ordinances and institutions, but minding His dispensations and the manner of His dealing with us. The ordinances of the gospel are from heaven, and not of men. Men have no right to institute who have no power to bless. Men's inventions in religion, though often followed with great eagerness, are found unprofitable and vain to them who have been zealous for them. But the ordinances which the Lord Himself has appointed, He is ready to own and make effectual to them who attend upon Him in the use of them, so that they shall have reason to say that they have sought the Lord and have found Him, and have tasted and seen that He is gracious. Ordinances are feasts with which saints are entertained, called by the prophet "feasts of fat things full of marrow, and of wine on the lees well refined" (Isaiah 25:6). And the people of God are so strengthened, revived, and delighted, and have such sensible communion with Him, that they speak out their joy and satisfaction. Verse 9: "Lo, this is our God: we have waited for him, and he will save us: this is the LORD; we have waited for him, we will be glad and rejoice in his salvation." Those are dangerously puffed up with pride and self-conceit who think that they are above ordinances; and 'tis not a commendable humility for them who desire the spiritual benefit of ordinances to imagine that ordinances are above them. They are in no wise to be neglected, for they are the "golden pipes" (Zechariah 4:12), that convey the grace of the Spirit into the hearts of men.

And as attenders upon God are found in the way of His ordinances, so they observe diligently God's dealing with them. They take notice how He looks upon them, whether there are smiles or frowns in His face; they regard what God speaks, whether it is by way of counsel, caution, rebuke, or comfort. They heed what the Spirit says to them, and what communications of grace are vouchsafed. They are attentive to regard the works of the Lord, and to consider the operation of His hands. Does He afflict? They turn to Him who smites them, and desire to be more fully instructed and more thoroughly purged (Isaiah 27:9). Does He load them with benefits? They are affected with His lovingkindness, and sensible how their obligations grow stronger to praise and please Him.

7. **Attending upon God implies expecting all from Him.** From this one Fountain flow the streams of all sorts of blessings. In our Father's house there is bread enough, and to spare; and however many are received and attend there, there is room for more—and not only room, but entertainment. The apostle, though he was as having nothing, yet had such a confident expectation from God as if he had all things in possession. 2 Corinthians 6:10: "as having nothing and yet possessing all things." He assured the believing Philippians that God would supply all their needs according to His riches in glory by Christ Jesus (Philippians 4:19). The psalmist, in danger and calamity, took himself to the mercy of God, and to the shadow of His wings for refuge; he cried unto Him as the most High, who performed all things for him (Psalm 57:1–2). Who questions whether the sun is full of light or whether the ocean abounds with water? Much less reason is there to question God's power and will to answer the expectations of His people who attend upon Him. It is His pleasure that they should wait upon Him for everything, and knock at His door, whatever they have to ask. Abounding in hope is acceptable to God, and will not issue in disappointment. Therefore David says in

Psalm 71:14, "But I will hope continually, and will yet praise thee more and more."

8. Attending upon God implies a readiness to do whatever He commands, and to engage at His bidding in any service. Nominal attendants will cry, "Lord, Lord," but real ones will do the things which He says. There are an innumerable company of angels who excel in strength, who wait on God, and those who do His commandments, hearkening to the voice of His Word (Psalm 103:20). That they may fulfill their Maker's pleasure, they minister to them who shall be heirs of salvation (Hebrews 1:14). Attendance includes a disposition to yield obedience. It is thus expressed in Psalm 119:48: "My hands also will I lift up to thy commandments, which I have loved." The lifting up of the hands shows a forwardness to receive whatever command God shall give, and a readiness to set about doing whatever He requires. This is becoming language: "Speak, LORD, for thy servant heareth." And he who is truly a servant will act according to what he hears his Lord speaking; and he will not give up though he is put upon the hardest and hottest service. Abraham rose early in the morning to obey God's command to offer up his son Isaac. The Lord swore to him by Himself because he had not withheld his son, his only son, from Him; He swore that in blessing, He would bless him (Genesis 22:16–17). 'Tis a temper of mind in which God delights, when His attendants resolve to obey without any exception. First Samuel 15:22: "Hath the LORD as great delight in burnt offerings and sacrifices as in obeying the voice of the LORD? Behold, to obey is better than sacrifice, and to hearken than the fat of rams."

9. Attending upon God implies giving glory to His Name, and acknowledging that His is the kingdom and the power. Though the offerings and sacrifices enjoined by the Law are

to be offered no more—Christ, who was typified by those sacrifices, having offered up Himself once for all, and put away sin by the sacrifice of Himself—yet, under the New Testament dispensation, attendants upon God have their sacrifices to offer. They must present themselves as living sacrifices, holy and acceptable to God, which is their reasonable service (Romans 12:1). And the apostle says in Hebrews 13:15, "By [Christ] therefore let us offer the sacrifice of praise to God continually, that is, the fruit of our lips giving thanks to his name." Those glorious spirits who attend above, and surround the throne in the heavenly kingdom, praise is their perpetual employment; and to their eternal joy and delight, they find perpetual reason for it. Worthy is the Lord to receive glory and honor and power; for He has created all things, and for His pleasure they are and were created. Worthy also is the Lamb that was slain to receive the same, and therefore "blessing, and honour, and glory, and power, be unto him that sitteth upon the throne, and unto the Lamb for ever and ever" (Revelation 4:11; 5:12–13).

This service of thanksgiving the Lord much insists on, is well pleased with, and accounts Himself glorified by. Psalm 113:1–3: "Praise ye the LORD; praise, O ye servants of the LORD, praise the name of the LORD. Blessed be the name of the LORD from this time forth and for evermore. From the rising of the sun unto the going down of the same the LORD's name is to be praised." Behold also how acceptable thankful attendants are. Psalm 69:30–31: "I will praise the name of God with a song, and will magnify him with thanksgiving. This also shall please the Lord better than an ox or bullock that hath horns and hoofs." And this is our way of glorifying God, who is so infinitely glorious that to His glory no addition can be made, but only a declaration and acknowledgment made of it. And when these acknowledgments are largest, it must be confessed, He is exalted above all blessing and praise.

10. Attendance upon God implies continuing to follow Him. Holy David says that his ears were opened, or bored, to hearken to God's voice (Psalm 40:6). Here is an allusion to the Israelite servant who was treated so well in his master's house that he refused to go out free at the year of release and had his ear bored with an awl to the post of the door to signify his resolution to serve his master continually. To profess service to the Lord, and then to depart from Him, is to highly reproach and dishonor Him. It is in effect to say that fleshly and worldly lusts are better lords than He; 'tis to more notoriously despise Him, and to harden others in their contempt of Him, and of His Word and commandments. Attenders upon God do not stop following Him in all those ways He has commanded them to walk in. They follow on to know Him; they follow Him fully and, being upheld with the right hand of His righteousness, their souls follow hard after Him (Psalm 63:8). And whom should they follow? To whom else should they go? The Lord has the words of eternal life. He alone has grace, honor, glory, and all other good things to give; and to go away from Him is to lose all this, and to tread the path which leads to eternal death. Attenders upon God cannot change their Lord without changing for the worse; nay, they exchange the very best for the very worst of all. Therefore they are unchangeably His, steadfast and unmovable, always abiding, and abounding in His work and service.

CHAPTER 3

Various Kinds of Attending upon God

Third, I am to speak of several sorts of attending upon God. It will be needful to insist particularly on these so that you may have a more distinct understanding of the extent and latitude of your duty. The Scripture makes a great difference between types of attendance upon God; so there are diverse kinds of it, as shall be manifested in these following distinctions. There is an attendance upon God which is with the lips and body only, and that which is with the heart also. I begin with this distinction to prevent hypocrisy and formality in religious duties, whereby the jealous God is so much provoked, and professors deceive others, but principally cheat and ruin their own souls.

1. There is an attendance which is with the lips and body only. God, by the prophet, spoke against this, and by His own Son shows the vanity of it, and how displeasing it is to Him. Matthew 15:7–8: "Ye hypocrites, well did Esaias prophesy of you, saying, This people draweth nigh unto me with their mouth, and honoureth me with their lips; but their heart is far from me." The body indeed is to give attendance, as being the temple of the Spirit. The tongue is then most angelic, and is man's glory, when it most enlargedly confesses to God, calls upon Him, and

praises and magnifies His name. But if when the eyes are lifted up towards heaven, the hands are stretched forth with great eagerness, the knees bow with seeming humility and devotion, and the words of the mouth are serious and holy, and with apparent fervency; if all this while the heart keeps aloof and at a distance from God, and does not value His love, His grace, or communion with Him, but goes after its pleasures, lusts, and covetousness—alas, here is only a dead and rotten carcass of a duty without a soul; and it is very loathsome and abominable. In all religious performances, if the heart does not at all care to draw near, it is certain that the Lord will not draw near either as to His gracious presence. And if God is not found in the duty, nor the heart of the performer found there, how unprofitable must the performance be!

There is an attendance upon God not with the body only, but with the heart also. He speaks unto us as unto children and says, "My son, give me thine heart" (Proverbs 23:26). Give Him never so much without this and you give Him nothing that He cares for. The heart does the chief part in the pure and acceptable worship of God. The heart must keep His commandments, or else they are not kept. Proverbs 3:1: "My son, forget not my law; but let thine heart keep my commandments." The psalmist lifted up his very soul to God (Psalm 25:1); this the Lord looked at and liked. Those graces which are to be acted in attendance upon God, such as faith and holy reverence, love, desire, and hope, and such like, are all seated in the heart; and 'tis by the heart that they are exercised. And when the heart, being cleansed from its defilements and weaned from the allurements of this world, draws very near to God, and God also draws very near—how reviving, how healing and confirming are these approaches! When the spirit of a saint does before the time, in a sense, return to God who gave it, and converses with Him in the heavenly places, how high, joyful, and beneficial is that converse found to be! When Moses came down from the mount where he had been with God, his face shone; and when the heart has been above in heaven, a clearer light shines into it, and 'tis more gloriously transformed into the divine image and nature.

2. There is also an attendance upon God that is voluntary, and another that is constrained and forced.

The attendance that is voluntary is when God, by His powerful grace, inclines and determines the will toward Himself so that He is chosen and His special favor and blessings are valued above all things. A mighty strength is put forth, and yet without coercion in bending the will of man toward God and to His will. The will of man is naturally so perverse and obstinate in evil that it is fitly compared to an iron sinew. What a power it is that can make it pliable! Psalm 110:3: "Thy people shall be willing in the day of thy power." And when the desire to will is thus wrought, the heart is then enlarged and at liberty to come to God and to do its duty. There is a renewed nature which is a principle of spiritual motion. This is notably expressed in Zechariah 8:21: "And the inhabitants of one city shall go to another, saying, Let us go speedily to pray before the LORD, and to seek the LORD of hosts: I will go also." The like temper we find in Jeremiah 50:5: "They shall ask the way to Zion with their faces thitherward, saying, Come, and let us join ourselves to the LORD in a perpetual covenant that shall not be forgotten.'"

There is an attendance which is constrained and forced. The heart is not right with God, nor taken with Him at all. But pressing necessity drives the soul to Him for some benefit which none but He can bestow. Or perhaps there are some indications of God's anger and displeasure, the effects of which they who attend on Him feel or fear, whereupon they are forced to cry for mercy. Such kind of attenders were those in Psalm 78:34–37: "When he slew them, then they sought him: and they returned and inquired early after God. And they remembered that God was their Rock, and the high God their Redeemer. Nevertheless they did flatter him with their mouth, and they lied unto him with their tongues. For their heart was not right with him, neither were they stedfast in his covenant." Had they not felt God's hand, He would not have heard their voice; had not their peril been extreme, they would not have run to this Rock for refuge; had not their enemies pressed hard upon them, they would not have cried to this high Redeemer for deliverance—but their cries were lies and flatteries. As soon as the danger was over (in their apprehension), their naughty hearts turned aside like deceitful bows, and they soon returned to their corrupt way. In attending upon God, do not let affliction, conviction, and fear of punishment be the only cords that haul you to your duty. The more there is of God's servant's will in his work, the more acceptable and well-pleasing is the service.

3. There is an attendance upon God that is ordinary, and one that is extraordinary. On one hand, as we are ordinarily to be employed in the works of our particular callings, so the works of our general calling, as we are Christians, must in no way be neglected. As we have bodies to feed and to clothe, and some business in the world to mind and manage, so we have souls to look after, and a God to serve—and this is the main business of all. To work out our salvation with fear and trembling is that which should always be upon our hearts. That man may truly say, "I have lost a day, if a day is gone and nothing at all of this work has been done." Mary is commended because she heard and heeded Christ's word, and, according to the direction of it, minded the one thing needful, and chose the

good part that could not be taken away from her. But Martha was taxed and reproved for being careful and troubled about many things (Luke 10:41–42). All the Lord's servants are to be attendants in ordinary things. Religion is to be the constant business of their lives, as being of greatest concern, and most worthy of their time and labor.

But there is also an attendance upon God that is extraordinary. When He goes out of the common way and course of His providence, His servants ought to follow Him. And as He acts extraordinarily in a way of judgment or of mercy, they are to do something extraordinary in the duties to which they have such a signal and loud call.

Acts of severity are called God's "strange acts" in Isaiah 28:21: "The LORD shall rise up as in Mount Perazim…that he may do his work, his strange work; and bring to pass his act, his strange act." Affliction is said to be strange either because His ordinary course is otherwise (kindness and mercy is what He delights in showing), or it may denote judgments that are unusual, and that have something more than ordinary terror and instruction. When the Lord is thus raised up out of His holy habitation, and comes forth to visit and punish iniquity, there should be great preparation to meet Him. Amos 4:12: "Because I will do this unto thee, prepare to meet thy God, O Israel."

There should be deep humiliation before Him. First Peter 5:6: "Humble yourselves therefore under the mighty hand of God, that he may exalt you in due time." There must be strong cries unto Him for pity, favor, and a spirit suited to His dealings. Psalm 18:6: "In my distress I called upon the LORD, and cried unto my God: he heard my voice out of his temple, and my cry came before him, even into his ears." Sin must be forsaken with more than ordinary sorrow and hatred as that which has provoked the Lord to be so very angry; and righteousness must be followed after with greater zeal and diligence. Isaiah 26:9: "When thy judgments are in the earth, the inhabitants of the world will learn righteousness."

On the other hand, when God acts extraordinarily in deliverance and salvation, songs suitable to deliverance should be loud; the heart should be exceedingly well tuned to praise His name. His attendants should call upon their souls, and all that is within them, to bless Him (Psalm 103:1). Love should be extraordinarily ardent unto God the Deliverer when extraordinary deliverance has been wrought. And He who is so mighty to save should be both feared and believed in together. Exodus 14:31: "And Israel saw that great work which the LORD did upon the Egyptians: and the people feared the LORD, and believed the LORD, and his servant Moses."

I might also add that when falls have been foul, and scandalous sins have been committed, then there should be extraordinary contrition and supplication to God for pardon and healing, for establishment by His Spirit, and for the joy of His salvation. When David, an eminent saint and prophet, suddenly turned black as hell, and became a monster of ingratitude, impurity, and cruelty, he came to God, being awakened by Nathan's ministry, with great shame and brokenness of heart (Psalm 51:16–17). He implored for mercy, begged for ease, and for the healing of his wounded conscience. He cried for a clean heart and a right spirit. And, being sensible of his own weakness, nay, treacherousness and unfaithfulness to himself, he entreated that the Lord would undertake for him, and by His own free Spirit continually uphold him.

4. There is an attendance upon God that is secret in the closet, private in the family, and public in the congregation.

First, there is an attendance upon God that is secret in the closet. Our Lord was much in prayer, alone by Himself, sometimes a great while before day and sometimes continuing in it all night. He commanded and urged secret prayer upon every one of His disciples. Matthew 6:6: "But thou, when thou prayest, enter into thy closet, and when thou hast shut thy door, pray to thy Father which is in secret; and thy Father which seeth in secret shall reward thee openly." God sees in secret, and hears even whispered confessions and petitions. And when it is said that He is in secret, it seems to intimate a special, gracious presence that is vouchsafed to them who are often alone with Him. In this secret attendance upon God, we may use a greater freedom of speech and tell Him all that we fear and feel, ail and desire. Secret duties that man can take no notice of do not have those motives that are very prevalent with hypocrites, who loved to pray standing in the synagogues, and by the intersections where two streets met, so that those in both streets might behold their devotions and applaud them. God is pleased to listen and hearken after prayer, and there is not the tiniest, homeliest corner where there is a sincere supplicant but God is really there to fulfill and grant the desire, and to support the burdened, if not to remove the burdens that are groaned under. Psalm 38:9: "All my desire is before thee; and my groaning is not hid from thee." And according to Solomon, "A gift in secret pacifieth anger: and a reward in the bosom strong wrath" (Proverbs 21:14), so secret confession of sin, bitter mourning for it, and begging forgiveness in the name of Jesus will prevail to pacify God's fiercest displeasure, and in obtaining His love and grace.

Second, there is an attendance upon God that is private in the family. This has been woefully, sinfully, and shamefully neglected not only by the profane, but by them who profess to be Christian, though they are hardly worthy of that name. Family worship has been much pressed from the pulpit. Oh, when shall it be that everyone's practice will be answerable to their profession? I read not only of a dedication of the tabernacle and temple, but also of the houses of the Israelites (Deuteronomy 20:5). Psalm 30 was composed at the dedication of the house of David. The Israelites justly called their houses God's houses. And those tumultuous, combined, and insulting enemies of theirs in pride, scorn, and derision said, "Let us take to ourselves the houses of God in possession" (Psalm 83:12). Houses were dedicated to the Lord's service. Joshua said, "As for me and my house, we will serve the LORD," and all Israel promised the same (Joshua 24:15, 21). David said that he would walk within his house with a perfect heart (Psalm 101:2), and that there would be songs of mercy and of judgment. Indeed, "The voice of rejoicing and salvation is in the tabernacle of the righteous" (Psalm 118:15). The Lord is adored and praised in the tabernacles of them to whom He has shown Himself to be a God of salvation.

Cornelius, one of the "first-fruits" of the Gentiles, was "a devout man; he feared God with all his house, and prayed to God alway" (Acts 10:2). Fearing God implies calling upon His name; as casting off fear and restraining prayer are joined together (Job 15:4), so this God-fearing man prayed unto God with all his house. There is not the least reason to think that they did not pray together unless such kind of praying had been anywhere forbidden. We read of a curse and a blessing not only upon persons, but upon families. Proverbs 3:33: "The curse of the LORD is in the house of the wicked: but he blesseth the habitation of the just." Surely families have reason to pray against the one, and that the other may rest on them. And truly our Lord Jesus, in that prayer of His own making, which is the great directory for prayer, when He instructs us to say, "Give us this day our daily bread," plainly signifies that those in families who daily eat together ought also daily to pray together. And are they only to pray together for daily bread? No, they are also to pray for the hallowing of God's name, the coming of His kingdom, and that His will might be done on earth as it is done in heaven. They are to pray for the forgiveness of past trespasses, and that grace may prevent their being led into temptation and deliver them from evil.

You see here ground enough for families to give their attendance upon God. Families are the seminaries from which both church and state are furnished; and if there were more of devotion, instruction, and discipline there, the church in all probability would be more pure, and the state more righteously and better ordered. Whereas, if families live without God in the world, the governors, the children, and servants are all usually wicked, likely to become worse and worse, and the church's face is fouled with odious spots and stains; and the state grows more corrupt until at length it is ripe for ruin.

Third, there is an attendance upon God that is public in the congregation. In public assemblies the true God is owned and honored in the face of the sun and the Lord Christ is glorified. Christians assemble in His name, depending upon His promise to be in the midst of them and to bless them. He walks in the midst of the golden candlesticks (Revelation 1:13). He blesses the ordinances that He Himself has instituted to the enlightening, purifying, and consolation of sincere attendants on Him. In these public assemblies, saints unite their spiritual strength in wrestling with God; the faith and holy desires of a great many believers being joined together are likely to prevail more. These assemblies ought to be valued and frequented; to forsake them is ill to the forsaker. Hence that caution in Hebrews 10:25: "Not forsaking the assembling of ourselves together, as the manner of some is; but exhorting one another: and so much the more, as ye see the day approaching." The breaking of solemn public assemblies should be a heartbreaking thing to us, and the Lord has promised to gather those who are sorrowful upon this score. Zephaniah 3:18: "I will gather them that are sorrowful for the solemn assembly, who are of thee, to whom the reproach of it was a burden."

5. There is an attendance upon God on His own day, and upon other days.

There is an attendance upon God on His own day. A seventh part of our time is hallowed by the Fourth Commandment. Six days are for labor; the seventh is for rest from that labor, and that we may have leisure, with greater seriousness, to attend upon God. The great Creator, having made the world in six days, rested on the seventh and appointed it as a Sabbath and blessed it. The apostle tells us that our Lord Jesus Christ, the great Redeemer, "is entered unto his rest," having "ceased from his own works, as God did from his." And therefore "there remains a rest [a keeping of a Sabbath] to the people of God" (Hebrews 4:9–10). As the Jewish Sabbath was kept in commemoration of the Lord's resting from creation, so the Christian Sabbath is to be observed in commemoration of Christ, who is over all, God blessed forever, and of His resting from the work of redemption. It is in Him that we have rest by faith at present, and hope for a blessed, glorious, and everlasting rest in heaven. The day when Christ rose was the day on which He rested; for His lying in the grave was not His rest, but part of His humiliation—and He rose on the first day of the week. On this day Christian churches assembled for worship (Acts 20:6–7). The Apostle Paul was at Troas seven days. We read not a word, as he was among Christians, that he solemnly worshipped on the seventh day, but "upon the first day of the week the disciples came together to break bread." Upon this day, Christians being assembled together, collections were made for good uses at Corinth, and in the churches of Galatia (1 Corinthians 16:1–2). Nay, this is called the "Lord's day" in Revelation 1:10. Now as the Lord's Supper is a supper of the Lord's institution, so the

Lord's Day is a day of the Lord's appointing and ordaining. The profanation of this Christian Sabbath has been punished with remarkable judgments. The ordinances administered thereon have been used and blessed to the conversion and confirmation of thousands and millions of souls.

On this Christian Sabbath, what kind of attendance on God should ours be! Before the day comes it should be longed for, and when it has come it should be most welcome. As soon as our senses are unlocked in the morning, our souls should be, as it were, caught up to the third heaven, and should there continue until night. Our Lord is risen indeed, and we should rise with Him and seek those things which are above, where He sits at the right hand of God (Colossians 3:1). Things on earth will be intruding into our hearts and thoughts, but no entertainment must be given to them. A desire or wish must not be allowed them unless it is that we may not be distracted with them. When Abraham came to Mount Moriah, he said to his servants, "Abide you here with the ass; and I and the lad will go yonder and worship" (Genesis 22:5). So when the Lord's day comes, we should say to all our worldly businesses and concerns, "Abide as you are; cease from our care and thoughts while we and our hearts ascend unto the hill of the Lord and worship." This day is appointed for our more solemn approaches unto God, and that we may have more intimate fellowship with Him. And if communion with Him is enjoyed, we shall find so much grace and strength and peace therein that we shall be perfectly of the psalmist's mind, that a day in God's courts is better than a thousand elsewhere (Psalm 84:10). The very palaces of the wicked are contemptible. No place under heaven is so desirable as the sanctuary.

There is also an attendance upon God on other days. He is the Lord of our time, and therefore He should have some part of each day. We should be careful to know how He would have us to employ that time which He gives, and for which He will call us to account. We should live the rest of our time in the flesh to the will of God, not to the lusts of other men, or our own (1 Peter 4:2); and we should grieve that so much has been wasted to His displeasure and dishonor. David was glad to go up to the house of God on the Sabbath; but He was also a daily attender on Him. Psalm 86:3: "Be merciful unto me, O LORD: for I cry unto thee daily." So it was with Heman in Psalm 88:9: "LORD, I have called daily upon thee, I have stretched out my hands unto thee." And Daniel, rather than omit praying daily unto God, ventured to be cast into the lion's den; and God miraculously appeared to Him, his mouth having been open so often in fervent supplication. God shut the lions' mouths so that, though Daniel was in the den among them, they did not make a prey of him. Every day we should be in the fear of God and have faith in Him; and if, in the midst of our worldly business, our hearts frequently step aside to attend on God in mental applications to Him, that attendance will be both acceptable and profitable. But some times every day we should sequester ourselves from other business so that this greatest and best business may be minded, which is to draw near to God.

6. There is an attendance upon God in a time of liberty and calm, and an attendance upon Him in a time of persecution and storm. In a time of liberty the Lord has many followers who leave Him when a storm of persecution beats in their faces. When the king of Navarre was about to apostatize to popery, and Theodore Beza came to confirm him in the truth, he replied that he would never go so far to sea as not to be able to put to shore when he pleased. He showed plainly that he could turn papist to get the kingdom of France, but he was resolved not to go through much tribulation to enter into the kingdom of heaven. The hearers compared to stony ground

heard the gospel with forwardness and joy, while the gospel and prosperity were conjoined; but when persecution and tribulation arose because of the Word, they were offended. They did not keep their standing, but in that time of temptation fell away (Matthew 13:20–21). We should be another kind of attendants than that. Let us count the cost of being disciples, and conclude that grace and glory will make up the cost. Our Lord was offended at nothing that was to be done or suffered for our redemption; surely neither His commands nor His cross should be matter of offense to us, but still we should remain His followers.

I might also add another distinction: there is an attendance upon God in earth and one in heaven; the one is duty, the other is reward; the one is short, the other is endless. And yet in that service there shall not be the least weariness; nay, so far from that, there will be fullness of joy and everlasting pleasure. Thus I have spoken of the several sorts of attending upon God.

CHAPTER 4

Why We Ought to Attend upon God

In the fourth place I am to assign the reasons why the children of men ought to give their attendance upon God.

1. The command to attend upon God is written on the heart of man by nature. There exists both creeds and the laws of nature. Some truths are apparent without a supernatural revelation, such as that there is a God, that He rules the world, that He sees all the works of the children of men, and that He will call them to an account for all that they have done. These commands are written in the hearts of men. Romans 2:14–15: "For when the Gentiles, which have not the law, do by nature the things contained in the law, these, having not the law, are a law unto themselves: which show the work of the law written in their hearts." And among these commands, this is as plain as any, that God is to be worshipped. The Gentiles therefore are blamed because this command was not observed. Romans 1:21: "Because that, when they knew God, they glorified him not as God, neither were thankful; but became vain in their imaginations, and their foolish heart was darkened." Now as sins have their peculiar aggravations that are committed against the light of nature, so neglect of duty is

highly aggravated when it is evident by the light of nature that such duty ought to be performed.

2. Attendance upon God is frequently called for and urged in the Scripture. The Lord spoke this with His own voice from heaven, and afterwards wrote it with His own hand upon the tables of stone, that we should have no other gods before Him, that we should not worship idols, that we should not take His name in vain (Exodus 20). Our Lord repeats what was enjoined long before. Matthew 4:10: "It is written, Thou shalt worship the Lord thy God, and him only shalt thou serve." And He says in John 4:24, "God is a Spirit, and they that worship him must worship him in spirit and in truth." So Psalm 22:23: "Ye that fear the Lord, praise him; all ye the seed of Jacob, glorify him; and fear him, all ye the seed of Israel." See also Psalm 105:3–4: "Glory ye in his holy name: let the heart of them rejoice that seek the LORD. Seek the LORD, and his strength: seek his face evermore." And as the Word of God calls for this, so the providence of God seconds His precepts. The dispensing of mercies calls upon us to attend the Father of them with our praises. Afflictions should also quicken us in our seeking God. He requires this in Psalm 50:15: "Call upon me in the day of trouble: I will deliver thee, and thou shalt glorify me." And He reckons upon it that He should hear from His people when His chastening is upon them. Hosea 5:15: "I will go and return to my place, till they acknowledge their offense, and seek my face: in their affliction they will seek me early."

3. God sees whether there is an attendance upon Himself, and after what manner, and that with a jealous eye. And this is another strong reason for our attending on Him. The Lord looks down from heaven upon the children of men, to the very end that He may see if there be any that understand and seek God (Psalm 53:2). So He very strictly observes how men's

hearts are affected toward Him and His service; and He cannot but be very much displeased with the whole race of fallen man because "There is none righteous, no, not one: there is none that understandeth, there is none that seeketh after God" (Romans 3:10–11). The Lord takes notice how days and weeks, and months and years go over men's heads, and yet that God from whom they have their all, they do not seek at all after. Neither do they return any thanks to Him, however much they receive from Him. And those who attend upon God, He observes the manner how they do it. Heartless duties, or doing the work of the Lord deceitfully, provokes and kindles the fire of His jealousy. Malachi 1:14: "Cursed be the deceiver, which hath in his flock a male, and voweth, and sacrificeth unto the Lord a corrupt thing."

The second commandment, which directs us as to divine worship, makes mention that the Lord is a jealous God. He cannot endure to have His service neglected, as if there were no profit or reward in seeking Him. He cannot endure a negligent service, as if He were an idol, as if He had eyes but did not see or take notice who they are who mock Him. God's omniscience and all-seeing eye struck a great awe upon the apostle; it made him draw near to God, and made him very serious when he had to deal with Him. Hebrews 4:13: "Neither is there any creature that is not manifest in his sight: but all things are naked and opened unto the eyes of him with whom we have to do."

4. Man's necessities should constrain him to attend upon God. Sin has made the children of men poor and needy in the worst sense. They fancy themselves rich, and dream of fullness; but, behold, 'tis only a dream, for they are wretched, miserable, poor, blind, and naked. Now for the supply of their needs, 'tis in vain to have recourse to any but God. The broken cisterns

can hold no water and cannot furnish them with any who run to them; but there is enough in the Fountain of living waters, for all who repair to it. An experienced attender upon God knew how to be furnished with everything. Psalm 57:2: "I will cry unto God most high; unto God that performeth all things for me." And the apostle speaks with a most reasonable confidence in Philippians 4:19: "My God shall supply all your needs according to his riches in glory by Christ Jesus." The one thing needful is from God alone, and from Him are all things else. His kingdom and righteousness He bestows on them who seek Him, and all things else shall be added (Matthew 6:33). Man has beggared himself; as to the true riches, he is a mere bankrupt. In man, that is, in his flesh, dwells no good thing (Romans 7:18), and that which is born of the flesh is flesh, wholly carnal, till there is a regeneration by the Spirit. How shall man, who is so very evil, be made truly good? All true grace and goodness is from God, who is therefore called the "God of all grace" in 1 Peter 5:10; and 'tis through Christ that it is all communicated. Therefore every good thing in believers is said to be in them in Christ Jesus (Philemon 6). Man has need to come to God for he has ruined himself, and it is the Lord alone to whom salvation belongs. Man has destroyed himself, but in God is his help found (Hosea 13:9). Those whom the Lord does not save must perish.

5. Man's obligations to attend upon God are still increasing. The Lord causes His sun to arise upon the evil as well as the good, upon the unrighteous as well as the righteous (Matthew 5:45). He is kind to the unthankful and the evil (Luke 6:35). God's bounty calls for a return of duty, and should quicken man to seek the Lord who is so abundant in goodness. Man's breath is in God's hand, and every time he breathes God saves his life. From God's hand he receives whatever he has. How

strictly is man engaged to acknowledge God in all, to serve Him and to glorify His name! Even those who are bad have experience of the riches of divine goodness, forbearance, and long-suffering. Though this goodness is but common, yet offers are made to them of special grace. All the day long the Lord stretches forth His hand to the disobedient and gain-saying; and in that hand are no less than the good things of time and of eternity. The most wicked and the worst of men, if they consent to leave their wicked ways, to have their wicked hearts changed, and to come to God, shall be graciously accepted and abundantly pardoned, with all the best things bestowed on them. God is ready to give grace to them who have none, and to give more grace where He has already wrought it.

6. The promises made to attenders upon God are precious, and the threatenings are terrible against condemners of God who refuse to attend upon Him. Thus the Lord works upon those two great commanding things in the soul of man, his hope and his fear, so that He may have service from him. If we draw near to God, He promises to draw near to us (James 4:8); and His approaches to His people are the manifestations of His pity and power for their help and supply, the communication of that grace which may be suitable and sufficient in the time of need. He says not to the seed of Jacob, seek ye Me in vain. Moses supposed Israel to be apostatizing from their God by idolatry; and his anger waxed hot against them, and they scattered among the nations. Yet he said, "If from thence thou shalt seek the Lord thy God, thou shalt find him, if thou seek him with all thy heart and with all thy soul" (Deuteronomy 4:29). Gracious words to the same purpose are sent in a letter to the captives in Babylon in Jeremiah 29:11–13: "For I know the thoughts that I think toward you, saith the LORD, thoughts of peace, and not of evil, to give you an expected end. Then

shall ye call upon me, and ye shall go and pray unto me, and I will hearken unto you. And ye shall seek me, and find me, when ye shall search for me with all your heart."

On the other hand, the God of truth and justice breathes out threatenings and wrath against them who despise Him; who, instead of seeking Him, turn their backs upon Him and forsake Him. Isaiah 1:24, 28: "Therefore saith the Lord, the LORD of hosts, the mighty One of Israel. Ah, I will ease me of my adversaries [they were a burden to Him, which at last He grew weary to bear], and avenge me of my enemies.... And the destruction of the transgressors and of the sinners shall be together, and they that forsake the LORD shall be consumed."

Sometimes God promises and threatens in the same breath, that He may prevail with man to come to Him and make him afraid to refuse. 1 Chronicles 28:9: "The LORD searcheth all hearts, and understandeth all the imaginations of the thoughts: if thou seek him, he will be found of thee; but if thou forsake him, he will cast thee off for ever." So Ezra 8:22: "The hand of our God is upon all them for good that seek him; but his power and his wrath is against all them that forsake him." And since the promised good and the threatened evil are thus presented together to our view, our hearts are more likely to be affected with the dreadfulness of the one and with the desirableness of the other.

7. The time will not last much longer in which God will be attended upon. Life is short, and death, which puts an end to man's life in this world, will bring the season of mercy and grace to an end. There is no passing through that great gulf which is fixed in the other world (Luke 16:26). Prayers in hell have no audience, but only a denial, though but a drop of water is asked for. Nay, the rich man could not prevail for any ease for himself, so neither for a messenger to be sent

to his surviving, secure, and sinful brethren to prevent their coming into the place of torment. Our Lord by His Spirit in the patriarchs went and preached to the spirits in prison; but it was before they came to that prison, even when the longsuffering of God waited in the days of Noah (1 Peter 3:19–20). When we read that admonition to "Seek ye the LORD while he may be found, Call ye upon him while he is near" in Isaiah 55:6, there is a plain intimation that quickly it may be impossible to find Him, and that to call upon Him may be too late and to no purpose. Despair hereafter will stop sinners' mouths and utterly discourage their crying unto God. Then they will call to the rocks and mountains to fall upon them and hide them from the face of Him who sits upon the throne, and from the wrath of the Lamb.

8. If man does not attend upon God, how much evil he will do and where he will go! If God has no service from him, sin and Satan will have much. Those who are not well employed in holy duties are likely to be very ill employed in the unfruitful works of darkness. The nature of man is so depraved that it has a mighty propensity to wickedness. And were it not for the grace of God, which either changes corrupt nature or chains it, what a universal running out would there be into all excess of riot, and with what greediness would iniquity be committed! But if God is not attended on and sought after, and if proud, scornful sinners would rather He keep His grace to Himself than bestow any of it upon them, He may justly leave them to the perverse bent of their own nature—and how sin will abound then! How will a wicked heart be perpetually sending forth polluted streams! Jeremiah 6:7: "As a fountain casteth out her waters, so she casteth out her wickedness." This is the way that the Lord punishes neglect of Himself and His service: He leaves men to themselves; and 'tis a very righteous and

proper punishment. Psalm 81:11–12: "But my people would not hearken to my voice; and Israel would none of me. So I gave them up unto their own heart's lust: and they walked in their own counsels." Being thus left to follow the counsels of a carnal mind and fulfill the lusts of a wicked heart, what a child of hell man may quickly become, and what haste he makes in going there! He may ripen quickly for ruin, and be suddenly destroyed, and that without remedy.

9. Attendance upon God is not profitable to God in the least, but man has the benefit and advantage by it. He was a man of eminent goodness whose soul said unto the Lord, "Thou art my Lord: my goodness extendeth not to thee" (Psalm 16:2). But though David's goodness did not extend to God, to draw near to God was good for David. Saints and angels, by their highest services, can add nothing to the Lord whom they serve. Their sublimest praises are an acknowledgement that they have their all from Him and in Him. The better we are, the better obedience we yield; but the Lord is not bettered by our best obedience. It is highly reasonable that we should attend upon God; for though He can receive nothing from us, yet He is ready to give Himself and all things to us if we seek Him diligently. He seeks our interest in His commands to come, to fear, to love, and to cleave to Him. Deuteronomy 10:12–13: "And now, Israel, what doth the LORD thy God require of thee, but to fear the LORD thy God, and to walk in all his ways, and to love him, and to serve the LORD thy God with all thy heart and with all thy soul, to keep the commandments of the LORD, and his statutes, which I command thee this day for thy good?" Man's good, you see, is aimed at—that in fearing God and keeping His commandments it may be well with him forever (Deuteronomy 5:29).

CHAPTER 5

Reproofs for Those Who Reject Attending upon God

USE OF REPROOF. Many sorts of persons deserve reprehension, and need it.

1. They are to be reproved who are haters of God, and who hate to attend upon Him. 'Tis prodigiously unreasonable that the gracious God who fills the earth with His goodness (Psalm 33:5), and is most worthy of the love of all, should be hated by any. Yet, though strange, 'tis too true that God is hated by many, nay, by most of the children of men. Most are of their father the devil, and the lusts of their father they will do; he is a hater of God, and so are his children. All wicked men are alienated from God, and enemies in their minds by wicked works. They dislike Him and His service; they get out of His ways and turn aside out of His paths, and say, "Cause the Holy One of Israel to cease from before us" (Isaiah 30:11). They neither care to hear nor to think of this Holy One; they cannot abide to walk in His holy ways. Now if love for God is the first and greatest command, how great a sin must the hatred of God be! And how unfit are they to be admitted hereafter into His glorious presence and kingdom who now say unto God, "Depart from us!" Most worthy they are to be sent away from Him with His curse, and to be sentenced to that everlasting

fire prepared for the devil and his angels, whom they resemble in their hatred of God, and with whom they have joined in rebelling against Him.

2. They are to be reproved who account attendance upon God needless. The mind of man appears to be void of judgment in determining what things are mainly to be minded. Things that are vanity and vexation of spirit, what pains are taken to get them; what care is taken to keep them! The one thing needful is neglected, as if it were the only thing unnecessary. The heathen poet cried out, "The care of man about empty things, how injudicious it is!" Time can be found for everything but making provision for eternity; and yet providing for eternity is the main thing to be done in time—and time was given chiefly to do this.

Are these to be our great inquiries: What shall we eat and drink, and wherewith shall we be clothed and adorned? How shall we heap up wealth, and gratify ourselves with sensual pleasures? How shall we live plentifully ourselves, and leave abundant substance to posterity? Certainly there are matters of far greater importance and necessity to be regarded.

The truly grand inquiries are of another nature. How shall sin be pardoned, and the wrath of God appeased? How shall the heart be changed and made a new one, and the soul that is so precious saved? How shall God be attended on, served, and glorified so as to be enjoyed, and eternal blessedness attained in the enjoyment of Him? Attendance upon God is no more to be counted needless than eternal happiness is, any more than the loss of a soul more valuable than the whole world is to be esteemed a small matter.

3. They are to be reproved who look upon attendance on God as a weariness, and as grievous. In following and trudging after mammon, they are unwearied. How swift and many are the

steps on the way to earthly delights and treasure! They rise up early, sit up late, rack their wits, grow lean with care for the things of the world, and do not begrudge at all this toil and labor. But when they come to wait upon God, time moves very slowly; a quarter hour seems longer than an entire hour. Duties are tedious to them; they are loath to begin; and as soon as they have begun, they do not wish for communion with God, or that they themselves might be bettered, but that their duties were at an end. The prophet was very sharp against them who despised the table of the Lord, who looked upon the fruit and meat of it as contemptible and said, "Behold what a weariness it is!" (Malachi 1:12–13).

God is weary of such unwilling services as yours are. Isaiah 1:13–14: "Bring no more vain oblations;…they are a trouble unto me; I am weary to bear them." And as He is weary of your services, so He quickly may be weary to bear you; and He may count it a comfort to be rid of you. Ezekiel 5:13: "Thus shall mine anger be accomplished, and I will cause my fury to rest upon them, and I will be comforted: and they shall know that I the LORD have spoken it in my zeal, when I have accomplished my fury in them." We read of some who were weary of Sabbaths. The ordinances they administered were to them no privileges, and "When will the Sabbath be gone?" was their language (Amos 8:5). But in verse 7, the Lord swears that He will not forget their works, and He threatens in verse 11 to send a famine in the land: "not a famine of bread, nor a thirst for water, but of hearing the words of the Lord." And how unlikely were they ever to be saved from whom even the means of salvation were taken away!

4. They are to be reproved who are sinfully ashamed or afraid to attend upon God. Some ages are so degenerate that religion grows exceedingly out of fashion, and contempt of God and

profaneness is the thing that is fashionable instead. When great men think it below them to be good and policy condemns piety; when the vilest men are exalted and wickedness grows in credit; when "judgment is turned backward and stands afar off; when truth has fallen in the streets and equity cannot enter, and he who departs from evil makes himself a prey" (Isaiah 59:14–15)—then this fear and shame that I am speaking against are apt to prevail.

But why should any be ashamed to own themselves as servants to the greatest and best of Lords? Is He not glorious in holiness? Are His precepts concerning all things not to be esteemed right? Are not all those ways false that lead away from Him? Has He not said, "Them that honour me I will honour, and they that despise me shall be lightly esteemed" (1 Samuel 2:30)? Christ will be ashamed of them at the great day who are ashamed of Him and of His Word before a perverse and wicked generation. And why should any be afraid to attend upon that mighty Lord who "doeth according to his will in the army of heaven, and among the inhabitants of the earth," when "all the inhabitants of the world are reputed as nothing" before Him (Daniel 4:35)? Attenders upon God should banish the fear of man, for God has evil men and evil angels in chains, and His sincere servants under His own keeping. Those who are afraid of man, who shall die, forget the living God and their duty toward Him, and how able He is to protect them in the faithful discharge of it.

5. They are to be reproved who attend upon God so that they may cover and cloak their wicked, worldly, and selfish designs. They put on a form of godliness, and 'tis the better to hide their wickedness. They are for external worship; but when they seem to seek after God most of all they are nothing but self-seekers, and religion is most unworthily made subservient to

secular interest. Thus the birds of prey, when they soar highest towards heaven, have their eyes still downwards toward the earth to see what they may seize on there. But what abominable hypocrisy is this, when love for the Father is pretended, but the thing intended is to gratify the lusts of the flesh, the lusts of the eyes, and the pride of life, which are not of the Father, but are of the world (1 John 2:16)! A cloak of religion is a specious and goodly thing to look upon. Praying, hearing, professing, singing of praises, presence at other ordinances, looking upwards toward heaven, and speaking like saints make the outside of this cloak. And, "Come see my zeal for the Lord of hosts," and, "The temple of the Lord, the temple of the Lord" make the cloak look still better outwardly. But the inside is most foul and filthy; there are found ambition, reprobate concupiscence, and insatiable covetousness. The purse must be filled, the palate must be pleased, the senses must be delighted, and pride must be gratified with applause and preferment. But certainly the Lord will not hold such dissemblers guiltless, who with such carnal designs take His name in vain.

6. They are to be reproved who are temporary attenders upon God, who in time of trial and temptation apostatize and depart from Him. Some kind of faint wishes they have that they might be saved, and with some kind of joy they entertain the glad tidings of salvation; but whatever becomes of their souls, their resolution is to sleep in a whole skin, and they will not hazard what they possess on earth for the sake of a treasure in heaven. The heat of persecution scorches such attenders as these, and causes all that is good in them to wither away (Matthew 13:6). They can by no means be reconciled to the cross of Christ, even though the Spirit of glory and of God rests upon those who take up this cross, and gives them a mouth and wisdom to

confound and silence the enemies of the truth, and strength to bear whatever wicked and unreasonable men can inflict, nay, abundant consolation when sufferings most abound. 2 Corinthians 1:5: "For as the sufferings of Christ abound in us, so our consolation also aboundeth by Christ." When these temporary followers of the Lord hear Him say, "If any man come to me and hate not [i.e., love less] his father and mother, and wife and children, and brethren and sisters, and his own life also, he cannot be my disciple," their answer is, "This is a hard saying; who can hear it?" And not enduring the trial and furnace is a sign that they are but reprobate silver which the Lord rejects. Their utter apostasy in the time of temptation shows that they never had root in themselves (Matthew 13:21). "If they had been of us," said the apostle, "they would no doubt have continued with us: but they went out, that they might be made manifest that they were not all of us" (1 John 2:19).

7. They are to be reproved who rest in the bare formality of attending upon God; but who do not desire or aim to reap any spiritual benefit thereby. Education, custom, and a regard for their reputation make them go in a road and round of duties—and hereby an ignorant, natural conscience has some kind of peace. But in all they do they have no eye on God, nor any sincere desires after Him. So ignorant are they of themselves that they are insensible of any spiritual necessities to be supplied; they are insensible of any lusts and passions to be mortified, of any plagues in their hearts to be healed. When we attend upon God, His approbation is principally to be minded. "He is a Jew, which is one inwardly…whose praise is not of men, but of God" (Romans 2:29). And God Himself is chiefly to be longed after. Psalm 42:1: "As the hart panteth after the water brooks, so panteth my soul after thee, O God."

But these formal attendants do not care about God's approval of them, neither do they desire communion with Him. As long as the work is done, they do not care how nor how little they are spiritually advantaged. The door turns upon the hinges to and fro, but still is where it was many years ago. So these professors come to ordinances and leave them no better than they were. They were, many years ago, proud, worldly, selfish, passionate, sensual, and slothful—and, oh, their sin and shame! They are so still, or more so than ever, notwithstanding all their religious services!

8. The very best are to be reproved that there are so many sins in their holiest things, and when they give their best attendance upon God. Though they are new creatures, yet much of the old man remains; though they are born of the Spirit, yet in part they are still carnal. And this flesh lusts against the Spirit so that they cannot do the things that they would (Galatians 5:17)—and what they do, they cannot do so well as they desire to do it. They are to be pitied indeed under their groaning because of indwelling sin. The apostle called himself wretched because of this, though he was joyful under the heaviest cross he ever bore.

And yet saints are to be reproved too because, were it not their own fault, they might still do and be better. They might have more grace from Christ, life more abundantly from Him; they might have more aid from the Spirit; they might be more enlarged in ordinances, and with greater swiftness run the ways of God's commandments. Even when they have done all, all is so defective that they have need of the perfect righteousness of Christ to cover their failings and imperfections.

CHAPTER 6

Exhortations for Those Who Reject Attending upon God

USE OF EXHORTATION. Let this exhort you all to attend upon God. Let not the world, and the god of this world, have you at their command; the things that their attendants take up with are a mere show, and are gone presently. The psalmist, speaking of those who mind only such things as these, with great asseveration tells us in Psalm 39:6, "Surely every man walketh in a vain show; surely they are disquieted in vain." And then he adds in verse 7, "And now, Lord, what wait I for? My hope is in thee." If he had expectations from the creature, he knew they would be frustrated; but hoping in God, he was well assured, would never make him ashamed.

The arguments to persuade you to attend upon God:

1. 'Tis wonderful condescension and compassion in God to admit attendance by such as you are. Whose eye but God's sees the whole of sin's evil? The Lord alone fully understands His own goodness, glorious perfections, and excellencies; therefore He alone fully understands sin's sinfulness, which is so contrary to Him. The psalmist tells us, He is not a God that hath pleasure in wickedness, neither shall evil dwell with Him (Psalm 5:4). When God prohibits sin, He speaks with great concern in Jeremiah 44:4, "Oh, do not this abominable thing

which I hate." You may perceive by His words that His very soul abhors iniquity.

'Tis therefore a matter of astonishment that God should have anything to do in a way of mercy with man who is so abominably guilty and defiled. What is there in man by nature to commend him to God? The apostle charges the whole world as guilty before God, and proves the heart, tongue, hands, and feet of man to be corrupt, and that "the way of peace have they not known" (Romans 3:17). Why should such a wretch be looked upon and graciously called upon to return? It is indeed eternal misery that man is in danger of, for divine mercy to prevent. Here is a great deal of sin for the justifying righteousness of a Mediator to cover; here are heart plagues for Christ, the Physician of Souls, to heal; here are stubbornness and obstinacy in evil for the Spirit of grace to overcome; here are innumerable wants for the all-sufficient God to supply—but not the least jot of meritorious worth. Will the Lord admit such as we are, indigent, worthless, and vile? Let us marvel that He will do it, and keep no longer at a distance from Him.

2. Remember that God refuses to be attended upon by multitudes of fallen creatures, who at first were better than man. We read that man was made a little lower than the angels (Psalm 8:5), so that the angels were in a degree higher than man in their first creation. Now a great host of these angels sinned, and when they sinned they were not spared (2 Peter 2:4); as soon as they fell into sin, they were thrown down and fell into hell. The Lord does not call out to the apostate angels to repent of sin and return to Himself. There is no throne of grace for them to come to, no mercy offered; the door of hope is locked up and fast barred against them forever. Our Lord did not take on Himself the nature of angels (Hebrews

2:16). The good angels were indeed confirmed in their good state, in their original integrity, by the Son of God, who is the Head of all principality and power (Colossians 2:10). But the Son of God redeemed and recovered not so much as one of the bad angels; rather they are all in chains of darkness reserved unto judgment. These reprobate angels are of very great capacity; they excel in strength, yet the Lord will accept no service at their hands. He forces them against their wills to be subservient to His purposes and pleasure, but worship and obedience from them He does not admit.

But He calls after man to return, though fallen by his iniquity (Hosea 14:1). He puts words into man's mouth and tells him what he should say, and what He Himself is ready to hearken to and grant. Hosea 14:2: "Take with you words, and turn to the LORD: say unto him, Take away all iniquity, and receive us graciously: so will we render the calves of our lips." This great difference which grace makes between fallen man and fallen angels should be a mighty inducement and encouragement to man to give a most ready attendance upon God.

3. 'Tis the great endeavor of your spiritual enemies to hinder your attendance upon God, or to disturb you in it, which shows that they are well aware how beneficial this attendance, if serious, would be; and they envy you the benefit of it. 'Tis wisdom well to mark and to receive some instruction from an enemy. What Satan urges you to pursue, you may conclude is of little worth; his malignity is such that he will not truly consider your interest. And since he uses so many methods, and so much subtlety, to stave you off from God, you may reasonably argue that in coming to God lies your duty and your blessedness. The enemy of our salvation has false glasses through which he misrepresents the Lord and His service to us. Sometimes he represents Him as so high that He does not notice what we

do, whether it be good or evil. Sometimes he sets Him forth as so indulgent that any careless duties will please Him, and that neglect of His service will not much, if at all, provoke Him. Sometimes he sets before man's eyes God's wrath and jealousy, and says that delays to serve Him have rendered Him unentreatable, and that to seek Him is now too late and in vain. Thus he would obstruct man's attendance on his Maker, for he knows that "the LORD is good to them that wait for him, to the soul that seeketh him" (Lamentations 3:25), and that those that are far from God shall perish (Psalm 73:27).

But if by all these ways he cannot hinder attendance upon God, he will endeavor to disturb them who do attend. Zechariah 3:1: "And he shewed me Joshua the high priest standing before the angel of the LORD, and Satan standing at his right hand to resist him." How busy is Satan about us when we come to appear before God! He endeavors to fill the mind with vain imaginations, to thrust violently the world into the heart, to make indwelling sin active, and to hinder the actings of grace. He endeavors to batter faith, to beat down hope, and to dampen holy and spiritual affections. He cannot endure that the soul should meet with God in duties; he is troubled at its communion with God and being blessed with spiritual blessings. But all this should but quicken your desires and diligence in seeking; for what you seek after, you may conclude is highly worth finding.

4. How empty are all things that are apt to draw you away from attending upon God! The Egyptians of old were derided by the poet because they made gods of everything. The very herbs and plants that grew in their gardens were deified. And truly, among many who are called Christians, a multitude of things that are very mean and low are idolized. Some make idols of their garbs by affecting and being proud of them. Some

idolize their earthly treasures and sensual pleasures by loving those more than God (2 Timothy 3:4). Some make their belly their god; and how many meat offerings and drink offerings are sacrificed to this base deity by the wine-bibbers and riotous eaters of flesh! How low man is fallen! How he has lost his dominion over the creature! They make him not only their slave, but their worshipper. But think with yourselves, and take notice what things they are that thus captivate and draw you away from God. Such is the immensity of God that the whole world, compared with Him, is not so much as the smallest dust to the globe of earth, nor so much as a drop of water to the whole ocean. And as the being of God transcends all other beings, so His goodness excels all created goodness. So that our Lord, speaking in the highest sense, affirms that there is none good but one, and that is God (Matthew 19:17). What then are the good things of this world that sin has brought a vanity, nay, a curse upon, and that are used by Satan as his great baits to catch inconsiderate souls that they may be lost and ruined?

5. Be prevailed with to attend upon God, who is the strongest Rock, the surest Refuge. Safety is desirable, considering what precious souls we all are entrusted with, and how full of enemies and snares this world is in which we live. But the Lord alone is He from whom safety comes. Psalm 18:31: "Who is God save the LORD? And who is a Rock save our God?"

Sincere attenders upon God are very dear to Him; they are called His "peculiar treasure" in Exodus 19:5: "Now therefore, if ye will obey my voice indeed, and keep my covenant, then ye shall be a peculiar treasure unto me above all people." They are called His jewels in Malachi 3:17: "They shall be mine, saith the LORD of hosts, in that day when I make up my jewels; and I will spare them, as a man spareth his own son that serveth him." Nay, he that toucheth them toucheth the apple of His eye (Zechariah 2:8). Therefore He will keep them as the apple of the eye. He will hide them under the shadow of His wings (Psalm 17:8). When you attend upon God, you repair to a Rock of salvation, to a high tower of defense. With His favor He will compass you as with a shield (Psalm 5:12). "He shall cover thee with his feathers, and under his wings shalt thou trust: his truth shall be thy shield and buckler" (Psalm 91:4). In the hollow of His hand you shall be hidden; and the same hand shall beat down all your enemies who design your destruction. You shall "dwell on high;" your "place of defence shall be the munitions of rocks" (Isaiah 33:16). No Rock is so high, so firm as God; no munition is so safe; the Refuge is eternal. When David says, "Unto thee will I cry, O LORD my rock; be not silent to me" (Psalm 28:1), it signifies that this Rock can hear, can answer, can help abundantly, and can afford abundant matter for thanksgiving. Psalm 18:46: "The LORD liveth; and blessed be my rock; and let the God of my salvation be exalted."

6. The God whom you attend upon can abundantly satisfy the very soul of man. When the soul has wearied itself with seeking satisfaction from the creature, and is sorrowful because its labor has been in vain, God can say and do what creatures cannot do. Jeremiah 31:25: "I have satiated the weary soul, and I have replenished every sorrowful soul." The negative happiness is considerable in being secured from evil and misery; but positive blessedness is more in being satisfied and delighted with divine goodness. Psalm 65:4: "Blessed is the man whom thou choosest, and causest to approach unto thee, that he may dwell in thy courts: we shall be satisfied with the goodness of thy house, even of thy holy temple." The rich man in the gospel speaks as if he had, like Nebuchadnezzar, the heart of a beast rather than the soul of a man when he

says, "Soul, thou hast much goods laid up for many years; take thine ease, eat, drink, and be merry" (Luke 12:19). This was but sorry provision for an immortal soul that was just ready to be required at God's hand, to leave all these things behind it and to go into eternity.

Attenders upon God find that in Him with which their souls are satisfied indeed. They are satisfied with His mercy and love in Christ. They are satisfied in Christ's sacrifice and the satisfaction He has made for iniquity. They are satisfied when they perceive themselves changed more and more into the image of God—and what a satisfaction is it to converse above, and to sit in heavenly places! Ephesians 2:6: "And hath raised us up together, and made us sit together in heavenly places in Christ Jesus." And what a satisfaction is it at present to be assured of a far fuller satisfaction hereafter! Psalm 17:15: "As for me, I shall behold thy face in righteousness. I shall be satisfied, when I awake, with thy likeness."

7. Attend upon God, for He has long waited that He might be gracious to you. How that Scripture in Isaiah 30:18 has been fulfilled: "And therefore will the LORD wait, that he may be gracious unto you; and therefore will he be exalted, that he may have mercy upon you." He has stood at the door and has knocked for entrance; and though that has been denied Him, He has not gone away as He might, in just anger, but behold, He stands at the door still (Revelation 3:20). If you hear His voice and open the door, He will enter and dwell with you, and He and His benefits shall be yours.

It is well for sinful man that God is patient and long-suffering. He does not cease calling at man's first deafness to His call. He does not cease offering grace, mercy, and life upon man's first refusing to accept what is offered. He told the old world that His Spirit would not always strive with man (Genesis

6:3), yet 'tis added, "his days shall be an hundred and twenty years." All that time the "long-suffering of God waited in the days of Noah, while the ark was a-preparing" (1 Peter 3:20), to see if the disobedient would return to Him. The Lord comes year after year to the barren fig tree seeking fruit, but He finds none, whereupon He says, "Cut it down; why cumbereth it the ground?" Yet when intercession is made, He is prevailed with to spare it longer, to see if means that were used might be effectual to make it fruitful (Luke 13:6, 9). The apostle tells us that "the Lord...is long-suffering to us-ward, not willing that any should perish, but that all should come to repentance" (2 Peter 3:9). Oh, repent of your forgetting God and your duty toward Him days without number; attend and seek unto Him in sincerity, who has had many a long look for you, and has waited so great a while for your return.

8. Consider seriously how God is attended upon in heaven, and what an honor it is to you to wait upon Him. He has thousand thousands that minister unto Him, ten thousand times ten thousand that stand before Him (Daniel 7:10). He has angels who excel in strength, who surround His throne, who are ready to do His commandments, hearkening to the voice of His Word (Psalm 103:20). The seraphim worship Him with covered faces to show their great reverence of God, and how they are ravishingly overcome with the brightness of His majesty; and they cry out one to another, "Holy, holy, holy, is the LORD of hosts; the whole earth [as well as heaven] is full of his glory" (Isaiah 6:2–3). These angels are spirits, these ministers likened to a flame of fire in Psalm 104:4. How sublime and spiritual are their praises! How ardent their love for the Lord whom they praise and serve! And yet the Lord is said to humble Himself when He takes notice of such attendants as these. 'Tis certainly a high honor that is done you when you

are admitted into the presence of such a glorious majesty. He who sits upon a throne of grace, and is so ready to pity, pardon, heal, help, and save, "is the blessed and only Potentate, the King of kings, and Lord of lords; who only hath immortality, dwelling in the light which no man can approach unto; whom no man hath seen, nor can see: to whom be honour and power everlasting. Amen" (1 Timothy 6:15–16). If this glorious God will accept service from such as you, how readily should you give it! How highly are you favored when you come into His presence and have communion with Him!

9. Lay this to heart, that not to attend upon God is wickedly to condemn Him and to rebel against Him. 'Tis in effect to say that He is not worthy of your service, and that the service of your lusts, and of the world, is more beneficial. Thus God was despised by those wicked men who were infatuated by prosperity in an evil way. They said in Job 21:15, "What is the Almighty, that we should serve him? and what profit should we have, if we pray unto him?" When Saul refused to obey the command of God, Samuel rejected his sacrifices and charged him with rebellion, which is as witchcraft, in 1 Samuel 15:22–23: "Behold, to obey is better than sacrifice, and to hearken than the fat of rams. For rebellion is as the sin of witchcraft, and stubbornness is as iniquity and idolatry." When you cast off the service of God, you cast off His fear and disown God Himself. This is rebellion, and this rebellion is your witchcraft, your confederacy with the devil. You make a covenant with death; you have reached an agreement with hell.

CHAPTER 7

Directions and Consolations for Attending upon God

USE OF DIRECTION. How should God be attended upon? There must be not only a seeking of God, but a due order in seeking Him. If this is wanting, instead of receiving benefits from His hand, that hand may make a breach upon us. First Chronicles 15:13: "The Lord our God made a breach upon us, for that we sought him not after the due order." If we have no care as to the manner of our services, the Lord will care as little for the matter of them. Now the right manner of attending upon God is to be declared in these particulars:

1. Our attendance upon God must be present; our living without God so long, and our contemptuous neglect of our required duty toward Him, should be matter of deep humiliation. And 'tis but reasonable to judge ourselves worthy of frowns and rejection because we sought His face no sooner. But now immediately we must gird up the loins of our minds to His work. The Holy Ghost bids us hear His voice today. He tells us that the accepted time is now. The psalmist is a pattern worthy of imitation for his present hearkening to the voice of God and his speediness in yielding obedience. Psalm 119:60: "I made haste, and delayed not to keep thy commandments." Delays are displeasing to God, for they argue the heart to be not well

reconciled to Him and to His precepts, and show that some other business is liked and preferred before His work. And these delays are dangerous, considering the uncertainty of our life's continuance, and how soon and suddenly the Spirit of the Lord, being grieved by our delaying to obey His motions and accept His gracious aid, may totally and finally withdraw from us.

2. Our attendance upon God must be instant. Romans 12:12: "Continuing instant in prayer." So Acts 26:7: "Unto which promise our twelve tribes, instantly serving God day and night, hope to come." When we are thus instant in our attending, it implies a sense of the great importance of those things we come to God about, and that we are very urgent with Him so that we may not miscarry in our everlasting concerns. Matters of life and death, though temporal, are managed with great seriousness.

But when we attend upon God, eternal life is before us to be laid hold on, and eternal death is before us to escape. Our intensity and urgency here should, if it were possible, as far exceed our seriousness in other matters as time in length is exceeded by eternity. As the loudest thunder drowns a whisper, so should the grand concerns of the unseen eternal world, when we come before God, be carefully regarded before the petty matters of this present life, which are but for a moment.

3. Our attendance upon God must be constant. Paroxysms and fits in religion argue an unhealthy soul; to be sometimes hot and sometimes cold is a bad temper. They who grow weary of God and of His service, God is weary of them and their duties. The Lord speaks to Ephraim and Judah as One wearied because all the means and methods He had used had been ineffectual unto any lasting reformation; if at any time they seemed inclined to what was good, the inclination was

very short-lived, and they soon returned to their natural bent and inclination to evil. Hosea 6:4: "O Ephraim, what shall I do unto thee? O Judah, what shall I do unto thee? for your goodness is as a morning cloud, and as the early dew it goeth away." It is not enough to begin well. The same argument that persuaded you to begin will become stronger for your holding on. It "had been better for them not to have known the way of righteousness, than, after they have known it, to turn from the holy commandment delivered to them" (2 Peter 2:21). All who come to God should cleave unto Him; all who embrace His testimonies should stick to those testimonies. "I have stuck unto thy testimonies," says Psalm 119:31; and verse 112: "I have inclined mine heart to perform thy statutes alway, even unto the end."

4. Our attendance upon God must be cordial and hearty. First Chronicles 22:19: "Now set your heart and your soul to seek the LORD your God." The full bent of the mind must be in this way. The Lord will not be found unless the heart and soul are set to seek Him. Naturally the heart of man is set in another way, being of a corrupt origin, estranged since the womb from God, and still it is further alienating and estranging itself. 'Tis not easy to have such a heart reconciled to God, and to the will of God. But when the heart is renewed, the enmity is in a great measure cured, and the heart is now willing to come into the Lord's presence; for when the heart serves Him, it is on the way to being satiated by Him. The Heart-searcher cannot bear the heart's absence; for if He does not have the heart, something else has it, which provokes Him unto jealousy. But the more there is of the heart in duties, the better pleased God is with them, and the performers find them in a spiritual sense more advantageous. When hearts knock at heaven's gate, the gate shall certainly be open. When souls thirst for God, they

shall not fail to find satisfaction. Psalm 63:5: "My soul shall be satisfied as with marrow and fatness; and my mouth shall praise thee with joyful lips."

5. Our attendance upon God must be with clean hands and a pure heart. James 4:8: "Draw nigh to God, and he will draw nigh to you. Cleanse your hands, ye sinners; and purify your hearts, ye double-minded." So Psalm 24:3–4: "Who shall ascend into the hill of the Lord? or who shall stand in his holy place? He that hath clean hands, and a pure heart." The gospel strictly commands good works; without these faith is dead and vain, and love is only a seeming fire. The apostle speaks with great vehemence in Titus 3:8: "This is a faithful saying, and these things I will that thou affirm constantly, that they which have believed in God might be careful to maintain good works." Our Lord owns them for His near and dear kindred who are doers of His Father's work and will. Matthew 12:49–50: "He stretched forth his hand towards his disciples, and said, Behold my mother and my brethren! For whosoever shall do the will of my Father which is in heaven, the same is my brother, and sister, and mother." Attenders upon God must not allow themselves to do evil. Fellowship with the unfruitful works of darkness and fellowship with God are inconsistent. First John 1:6: "If we say that we have fellowship with him and walk in darkness, we lie, and do not the truth." Unless there is a living for God, serving Him in ordinances is of no account with Him.

And as hands must be cleansed, so the hearts of attenders on God must be pure. The heart must not defile itself by regarding any iniquity so as to be unwilling to have it subdued. Psalm 66:18: "If I regard iniquity in my heart, the Lord will not hear me." Regarded iniquity will cry so loudly for a denial that prayer will find no audience. The heart must not pollute itself by love for the world; for if this love prevails, there can be neither any true love for the Father, nor any interest in the Father's love. First John 2:15: "Love not the world, neither the things that are in the world. If any man love the world, the love of the Father is not in him." The heart must consent to the crucifixion of all the affections and lusts of the flesh. It must not be double-minded, on and off with God, but steady and right with Him. Its resolution must be to be holy still, and its desire to be still holy more and more, to have holiness perfected in the fear of God.

6. Our attendance upon God must be with humility, fear, and faith, without wrath and doubting. Humility becomes the very angels, for all their excellence is derived from God and even they are charged with possible folly (Job 4:18). 'Tis owing to the election and confirming grace of God that some angels stood, while others, being left to the freedom of their own will, apostatized. How humble should the children of men be who are fallen by their iniquity! The best of saints have reason to be low in their own eyes, considering how many talents they owed before they were satisfied for and paid for by their Surety, and how apt they are still to trespass. It may be said of the strongest Christian that he could not stand, and he would not stand, were he not upheld by the Lord's free and mighty Spirit.

But a humble sense of our worthlessness and ill-deserving should not hinder the acting of our faith in Jesus when we come before the Lord. Our great Redeemer has bought us with a price, and He has bought all things for us. We ourselves are His purchase, and so is all that grace we need, and all that glory we hope for. God has made a covenant with Christ, and has promised to give us to Him for His inheritance and possession. Psalm 2:8: "Ask of me, and I shall give thee the heathen for thine inheritance, and the uttermost parts of the earth for thy possession." And to be Christ's inheritance and possession implies our being separated from the world, our being secured, our being made fruitful, and our eternal continuing to be enjoyed by Him, and to enjoy Him. Promises of all blessings, and especially of the best blessings, are made to us for Christ's sake, and He will see to making them good because the accomplishment of them is so much for the Father's glory as well as our truest welfare. All this may exceedingly strengthen and raise our confidence and hope when we attend on God.

Doubts concerning our condition should be looked upon as unreasonable when we come in such a prevailing name as Christ's, unto His Father and our Father, His God and our God, and we ask only for things agreeable to His will. First John 5:14–15: "And this is the confidence that we have in him, that, if we ask any thing according to his will, he heareth us; and if we know that he hear us, we know that we have the petitions that we desired of him."

As faith is opposed to doubting, so it is opposed to wavering. James 1:6–7: "But let him ask in faith, nothing wavering. For he that wavereth is like a wave of the sea, driven with the wind and tossed. For let not that man think that he shall receive any thing of the Lord." He is the wavering man whose mind hangs doubtful and unresolved between God and the world, Christ and Satan, sin and holiness. Such an attender upon God, who is more inclined to serve other lords, shall certainly be rejected.

Finally, the apostle forbids not only doubting, but wrath also. First Timothy 2:8: "I will therefore that men pray every where, lifting up holy hands, without wrath and doubting." The wrath of man does not work the righteousness of God; nay, it causes an abounding in transgression. The leaven of anger and malice is diligently to be searched for and purged out as that which, if it remains, will prove us to be carnal. First Corinthians 3:3: "For whereas there is among you envying, and strife, and divisions, are ye not carnal, and walk as men?" Civil discords, church divisions, and unruly passions, should be avoided with care and fear; we should be full of holy love toward all our brethren, ready to forgive the greatest injuries and enemies, forward to pursue and promote unity and peace, whenever we attend upon Him who has called Himself the God of love and peace.

7. Our attendance upon God should be with gladness and delight, and a sense of how good it is for us to approach His presence. Where the will of God is best done, and that is in heaven, there is the greatest joy in doing it. The cheerful, joyful servant is a credit to his work, honors his Lord, and is a great eyesore to the evil one; for Satan is very much afraid lest the attenders upon God, being full of gladness, others should be induced to try that work and service which these find so exceedingly comfortable. Hypocrites, who go no further than the outside of religion, count it wearisome because they do not understand it. But as God takes pleasure in the upright, so the upright find the truest pleasure in God and in His ways.

The psalmist speaks upon very good ground in Psalm 32:11: "Be glad in the LORD, and rejoice, ye righteous: shout for joy, all ye that are upright in heart." The man after God's own heart said that the meditations of God are sweet (Psalm 104:34). He was glad when they said to him, "Let us go into the house of the LORD" (Psalm 122:1). He tells us which man will have all his desires granted: 'tis he whose delight is in God. Psalm 37:4: "Delight thyself also in the LORD; and he shall give thee the desire of thine heart." He is the blessed man who takes no pleasure in the counsel, way, or seemingly easiest seat of the wicked, but whose delight is in the law of the Lord (Psalm 1:1–2). And why should He not be served with delight at present since in His kingdom He will be praised by all with the highest rapture of joy forever!

8. Our attendance upon God should be in all ordinances. It is produced as an argument that that excellent couple mentioned in Luke 1:6 were both righteous before God because they walked in all the commandments and ordinances of the Lord blamelessly. Under the Old Testament there was an ordinance of God that was to be administered quickly to the infants, and that was circumcision; and though Abraham, at the first institution of this ordinance, believed and was circumcised in adulthood, as also were the men of his household; and though circumcision is called a "seal of the righteousness of faith" in Romans 4:11, yet infants also were circumcised. These little ones are said to enter into covenant with the Lord their God in Deuteronomy 29:11–12. Under the New Testament our Lord Jesus does not cast these infants out of His church and covenant, but says, "Suffer the little children to come unto me, and forbid them not: for of such is the kingdom of God" (Mark 10:14). The Apostle Peter, after he had exhorted to baptism, said, "The promise is unto you, and to your children" (Acts 2:39). And the Apostle Paul affirms that the children of believing parents are holy (1 Corinthians 7:14), and are therefore members of the body of Christ. Now it is plainly signified that baptism is the privilege of all in that body. First Corinthians 12:13: "We are all baptized into one body."

Indeed, some who mind the sound of Scripture more than the sense of it, when they read, "Repent and be baptized," or "Believe and be baptized," conclude that none but those who are of age and are capable of professing their faith and repentance ought to partake of this ordinance. But they would do well to consider who these were who in Scripture repented, believed, and were baptized: they were either Jews or heathens who were converted to the Christian faith as adults. If thousands of such should be converted now, now also, as adults, baptism ought to be administered to them upon their repenting and believing. But in the whole New Testament we do not find any baptized as adults whose parents were Christians at their birth. Yet several without Scripture warrant are thus baptized at this day.

Oh, that there were less disputing about infant baptism, and more care to apply it! All infants who go to heaven are baptized with the blood and Spirit of Christ; they are justified and sanctified thereby. This justification and sanctification all who have been baptized should desire to partake of.

Other ordinances also should be engaged in, for the Lord who has instituted them is ready to own and bless them, and to be found in them. Who that is wise would neglect any one of them, since none of them are appointed in vain? Nay, every one of them has been experienced by serious believers as abundantly beneficial. The Lord is to be attended upon, however and in whatever way He pleases—in the closet, in the family, in the sanctuary, at the table, or in any other way that He has ordained. "Blessed are all they that wait for him."

9. Every attendance upon God should make every attender better. 'Tis thought by some that creatures in the waters, as long as they live, grow still larger. Saints, as long as they live, should still be growing in grace and be more full of all goodness. They should grow as the lily, and cast forth their roots as Lebanon; their branches should spread, and their beauty should be as the olive tree (Hosea 14:5–6). God is ready to be as the dew to them, who from Him their fruit may be found. It is really a fault in believers if every time they wait upon the Lord they do not come away from Him with more wisdom, strength, grace, and peace than they had before since He is ready to

impart such blessings as these, and gives them liberally without upbraiding.

USE OF CONSOLATION. Let this console them who thus, as I have directed, attend upon God. Isaiah 40:1: "Comfort ye, comfort ye my people, saith your God." With joy you may come and draw most pure and refreshing waters out of the wells of salvation. You are the children of peace, and the peace of God is to rest upon you. For your comfort take notice of these things:

1. God puts a high value upon His sincere attendants. He had a special respect for Abel and the excellent sacrifice he offered. Though the heaven is His throne and the earth His footstool, yet to that man will He look, as being well pleased with him, who is poor and of a contrite spirit, and who trembles at His Word (Isaiah 66:1–2). He remembers "the kindness of thy youth, the love of thine espousals" (Jeremiah 2:2), and their willing consecration of themselves to be "holiness unto the LORD." He has taken notice of all their desires and groans, their cries to Him, and their frequent speaking one to another that they might confirm and encourage one another, in the worst of times and trials, to continue to be His attendants still. Malachi 3:16: "Then they that feared the LORD spake often one to another: and the LORD hearkened, and heard it." And He so well approved of them that a book of remembrance was written before Him, "for them that feared the LORD, and that thought upon his name."

2. God delights over His sincere attendants to do them good. He takes pleasure in the prosperity of His servants; they are in heaviness by affliction only when there is need of it. He delights especially to see their souls prosper. As He opens His armory and brings forth the weapons of His indignation against the

wicked, so He opens His treasures of bounty and goodness to His servants so that they may be supplied abundantly. He does them good with a good will. His whole heart and soul are with them (Jeremiah 32:41) when His hand is open to them. He is ready to fulfill their desires, to grant their requests. Nay, when their thoughts are most comprehensive and they crave never so much, He is able and ready to do for them exceeding abundantly more (Ephesians 3:20). Who can conceive how beneficial waiting upon God is! That passage is both encouraging and amazing in Isaiah 64:4: "For since the beginning of the world men have not heard, nor perceived by the ear, neither hath the eye seen, O God, besides thee, what he hath prepared for him that waiteth for him."

3. God is ready to cover a multitude of infirmities in them who sincerely attend upon Him. He mercifully observes how willing their spirits are when their flesh is weak and cannot keep pace with their renewed minds. When our Lord was in agony, His disciples could not watch with Him one hour, but had fallen asleep; yet He Himself graciously excused it, as we read in Matthew 26:41, "The spirit indeed is willing, but the flesh is weak," and He passed it by. He takes notice of the lustings of the spirit against the flesh, the strivings of grace against sin and corruption, and passes by the lusting of the flesh against the Spirit, the strivings of sin against grace. The Lord does not enter into judgment with His servants, nor deal in rigor with them, but He expresses fatherly tenderness and compassion toward them. Psalm 103:13: "Like as a father pitieth his children, so the LORD pitieth them that fear him." We are directed to beg for the forgiveness of trespasses daily, which shows that, as the disciples of Christ daily offend, so their heavenly Father is ready to grant forgiveness daily to them. Nay, iniquity cleaves unto our holiest things; our best duties

should and might be done a great deal better. These infirmities then are much to be lamented, more and more striven against; and seeing ourselves compassed about with them, we should banish all self-confidence and look unto Jesus, that in Him we may find acceptance. And certainly the righteousness of Christ, the Son of God, and the Father's love in Him will cover the great multitude of bewailed infirmities and offenses.

4. It may also comfort attenders upon God to think whom they have attending upon them. Saints on earth have the angels in heaven to be their guardians. Christ is signified by Jacob's ladder; the angels of God are said to ascend and descend upon the Son of man (John 1:51). 'Tis owing to our Lord Jesus that believers have the benefit of the angels' ministry, and the apostle signifies that all of them are thus employed for the saints' protection and security. Hebrews 1:14: "Are they not all ministering spirits, sent forth to minister for them who shall be heirs of salvation?" The reprobate and evil angels resist attenders upon God; but the elect and good angels are their friends. These angels who excel in strength, how they rejoice when any repent and are converted! And they have a charge over converts to keep them in all their ways (Psalm 91:11). And when it is added in verse 13, "Thou shalt tread upon the lion and adder: the young lion and the dragon shalt thou trample under feet," it may be intimating that Satan's force, fury, and subtlety shall be ineffectual, and that by his temptations he shall not prevail.

But though angels attend the servants of God, those servants are not entrusted solely to the angelic care. The Lord Himself is their Keeper. The Father and the Son come to them and make their abode in them, and will secure their own mansions till they are out of the reach of enemies and past all danger.

5. Sincere attendants upon God shall attend upon Him after another and better manner in another world. The attendants shall be fitted for and admitted into the presence chamber of the King of glory. In heaven there will be "no need of the sun, neither of the moon, to shine in it: for the glory of God did lighten it, and the Lamb is the light thereof." And "there shall be no more curse: but the throne of God and of the Lamb shall be in it; and his servants shall serve him" (Revelation 21:23 and 22:3). They shall serve Him so as never in the least to disserve Him; they shall do His will, and nothing at all contrary to it; there will be a perfection of delight, rest, and peace; in obedience they shall yield, when they "rest not day and night," saying, "Holy, holy, holy, Lord God Almighty, which was, and is, and is to come" (Revelation 4:8). And Revelation 5:13: "Blessing, and honour, and glory, and power, be unto him that sitteth upon the throne, and unto the Lamb for ever and ever!" All God's sincere attendants are now advanced to priestly, nay, to kingly dignity; therefore they are called a royal priesthood in 1 Peter 2:9. Christ has loved them and washed them from their sins in His own blood, and has made them kings and priests unto God and His Father (Revelation 1:5–6). But hereafter they shall inherit and possess the kingdom prepared for them; they shall all be actually crowned with a crown of life and righteousness. And, oh, what a joyful sight will it be to behold the Lord, and all His saints glorified together with Him! Colossians 3:4: "When Christ, who is our life, shall appear, then shall ye also appear with him in glory."

PART TWO

Attending upon God Means We Should Look upon Him as Lord and Serve Him

CHAPTER 8

How God Is the Lord

DOCTRINE 2. In attending upon God, we should look upon Him as the Lord, and serve Him accordingly. When God pronounced His own laws with His own mouth upon Mount Sinai, He thus began, "I am the LORD" (Exodus 20:2); and this was to awe Israel into obedience. We read in Deuteronomy 6:4: "Hear, O Israel: The LORD our God is one LORD." No other Lord is His equal; no commands are to be regarded like His commands. None is so worthy of service as He. He must have attendance, whoever or whatever else is neglected. Psalm 89:6–7: "Who in the heaven can be compared unto the LORD? who among the sons of the mighty can be likened unto the LORD?" The mightiest monarchs upon earth, the highest angels in heaven, are infinitely below Him; therefore it follows, "God is greatly to be feared in the assembly of the saints, and to be had in reverence of all them that are about him." Holy David cried out in Psalm 8:1: "O LORD our Lord, how excellent is thy name in all the earth! who hast set thy glory above the heavens." He worshipped and praised Him as the highest Sovereign, who excelled all things on earth and whose glory the heaven, though full of it, was not able to contain. And when he said "our Lord," it intimated that he was truly His servant and subject, and that he gloried in subjection to Him.

In the handling of this doctrine I shall:
First, show you how God is the Lord.
Second, manifest what influence and effect the apprehension of His being Lord should have upon us when we attend upon Him.
Third, and last, make application.

First, I am to show you how God is the Lord. His majesty may amaze us; when we think or speak of His dominion, we should be struck with godly fear. Thus it was with the psalmist in Psalm 104:1–2: "O LORD my God, thou art very great; thou art clothed with honour and majesty. Who coverest thyself with light as with a garment." Psalm 96:4, 6, 9: "For the LORD is great, and greatly to be praised: he is to be feared above all gods. Honour and majesty are before him: strength and beauty are in his sanctuary. O worship the LORD in the beauty of holiness: fear before him, all the earth."

Now, that you may better understand with whom you have to do when you attend upon God, you must know:

1. *God is Lord Creator, of whom are all things.* The man of God, Moses, with wonder and adoration cried out in Psalm 90:2: "Before the mountains were brought forth, or ever thou hadst formed the earth and the world, even from everlasting to everlasting, thou art God." The Lord was before all, and He was all, of, in, and to Himself from eternity. The Father is of Himself alone; the Son is necessarily and eternally of the Father; and the Holy Ghost as necessarily and eternally from both the Father and the Son. And these Three are that one living and true God in whom Christians believe, and in whose name they are baptized. But though God necessarily is, yet creatures are not so; rather they have their being at His pleasure. Revelation 4:11: "Thou art worthy, O Lord, to receive

glory and honour and power: for thou hast created all things, and for thy pleasure they are and were created."

It is the Lord whose word of power and command brought all things out of nothing at first. Hebrews 11:3: "Through faith we understand that the worlds were framed by the word of God." Though some have imagined that angels were created, and many of them fell, long before this visible world was made, in Scripture there is no sufficient ground for such an imagination. It is probable that those excellent creatures were made the first day, when 'tis said in Genesis 1:1, "In the beginning God created the heaven." The heaven may take in the highest heaven, and the host of angels there. Oh, what a powerful word was that which commanded angels to be, who before were nothing, and gave them spiritual and immortal natures, endued with such mighty strength and understanding! And when the Lord laid the foundations of the earth and stretched the line upon it, these glorious angels, called morning stars, sang together, and all these sons of God shouted for joy (Job 38:4–5, 7).

The Lord Creator did but say, "Let there be light," and there was light. The sun, the moon, the stars, the earth and seas, and all their hosts were what His Word made them. And man, who was to have dominion over this lower world, God made in His own image. His body indeed was formed of the dust of the ground; but to show that his soul was not of earthly origin, God is called the Father of man's spirit. He "breathed into his nostrils the breath of life, and man became a living soul" (Genesis 2:7). This great Creator whom we attend upon made all things very good (Genesis 1:31), and though sin entered into the world and spoiled much of His workmanship, He can easily make new what sin has marred, and He can easily and will certainly destroy those who are finally unwilling to be made new creatures.

2. God is Lord Preserver of what He has made. The word of His power sustains all things (Hebrews 1:3). It continues things in those beings into which at first it brought them. Psalm 148:5–6: "Let them praise the name of the LORD: for he commanded, and they were created. He hath also stablished them for ever and ever. He hath made a decree which shall not pass." The same Lord who called things out of nothing by His word hinders their returning into nothing by the same word of command. Psalm 33:9: "For he spake, and it was done; he commanded, and it stood fast." There is so much power exerted in upholding the creation that the preservation of the universe is rightly called a continued creation of it. If God should totally draw back His supporting hand, all the luminaries in heaven would presently lose their light; the earth and seas would become a chaos of confusion; nay, men and angels, and all things else, would immediately lose their being and become nothing.

As the creation is of the Lord alone, so is the preservation of all things. Nehemiah 9:6: "Thou, even thou, art LORD alone; thou hast made heaven, the heaven of heavens, with all their host, the earth, and all things that are therein, the seas, and all that is therein, and thou preservest them all." How worthy is He to be worshipped by the host of heaven, and by the sons of men, the inhabitants of the earth! God is called "Almighty" or "all-sufficient." All creatures, from the mightiest to the very meanest, hang and depend upon God as children do upon the breasts, that He may nourish and sustain them. And if God thus upholds all things, surely He will not fail to preserve His church and saints; they may with confidence attend upon Him for defense, for no human nor hellish force shall prevail against them.

3. God is Lord Proprietor and Possessor of heaven and earth. So Melchizedek called Him the most high God when he

blessed Abram, the father of the faithful, in Genesis 14:19: "Blessed be Abram of the most high God, possessor of heaven and earth." In Psalm 24:1 we read: "The earth is the LORD's, and the fullness thereof; the world, and they that dwell therein." All persons and things are properly God's own, and He may do with them what He pleases. By creation the Lord began, and by preservation He continues, to be the Proprietor of all things. Propriety is the ground of power, and power is the ground of government; and a most absolute and universal propriety and power the Lord rightly claims for Himself. He is accountable to none, and is not to be resisted by any. None can stay His hand or say to Him, "What doest Thou?" It was a good answer that Elihu made to Job in Job 33:12–13: "God is greater than man. Why dost thou strive against him? for he giveth not account of any of his matters."

It is a wise part to attend upon God, who has ownership of us and all things besides. All things are really in His hands and possession, so that He can withhold or bestow them according to His own will. If God is for us, He can make all things for us; if He is against us, nothing shall be for our help or benefit. There is nothing that we need but a super-abundance of it is in God's hand. The Possessor of heaven and earth has the blessings of heaven and earth to give forth. "Every beast of the forest is mine, and the cattle upon a thousand hills" (Psalm 50:10)—all sheep and oxen, yea, the beasts of the field, the fowl of the air, the fish of the sea, and whatever passes through the paths of the seas. How easy is it for Him to provide things of this nature, who has so much, who has all of them in His own keeping? But far better blessings than these He has in His hand to bestow; and of the best blessings He is most liberal. When we knock at His door, we should remember how rich He is, whose all things are; and that this Lord over all is rich unto all who call upon Him (Romans 10:12).

4. God is Lord Redeemer of His people, and a mighty Lord indeed He shows Himself in redeeming them. Jeremiah 50:34: "Their Redeemer is strong; the LORD of hosts is his name: he shall thoroughly plead their cause, that he may give rest to the land." Redemption supposes that the redeemed ones were enslaved, lost, and under a curse. To redeem must be granted to be a high act of mercy and grace, and of force and might likewise. The Lord is a Redeemer by power and conquest. He throws down the dominion of sin, demolishes its strongest holds, thrusts mammon out of the throne of the heart, and treads Satan under His people's feet.

In a sense, He is also a Redeemer by commutation. God became man that He might stand in man's place, suffer in man's nature, and be man's Surety and Savior. He redeems by paying a price, and that the price might be of infinite value, He gave no less than Himself for those whom He has redeemed. First Corinthians 6:20: "Ye are not your own, for ye are bought with a price: therefore glorify God [who bought you] in your body, and in your spirit, which are God's." In Galatians 2:20 the apostle says, He "loved me, and gave himself for me." The prey and the captives are delivered out of the hands of that terrible enemy, the prince of darkness. Believers are redeemed from the curse of the law by Him who was made flesh, sin, and a curse for them. They may triumph indeed because the first death is unstung, the grave has lost its victory, and none of them shall be seized and hurt by the second death. How should this Lord Redeemer be attended upon! How should sinful and lost souls, before they are past recovery, being sensible of their danger, come flocking to Him in great numbers, flying as a cloud, and as doves to their windows!

5. God is Lord and Lawgiver, and all are bound to obey the laws He gives them. His laws are the best that ever were given.

In the keeping of these laws lies true goodness; and sin, which is incomparably the foulest, most pernicious, and worst of all evils, is a transgression of these laws that God has delivered to us. How often in the New Testament do we read of the kingdom of God! The word "kingdom" implies a king and laws, and that there are subjects who must obey both. The cross of Christ does not exclude Christians' sufferings, but their sufferings are not expiatory of sin, as His were. And the obedience of Christ does not exclude Christians' obedience; but His was meritorious, and theirs is not. However strictly some may take the gospel, and say 'tis all promises, I am sure that the gospel, as it represents itself, includes commands. Christ is a King to be obeyed as well as a propitiatory sacrifice to be rested on; and He is the Author of eternal salvation to all who obey Him (Hebrews 5:9). The phrase "obey not the gospel" shows that there are laws to be obeyed; and they who do not obey "shall be punished with everlasting destruction from the presence of the Lord, and from the glory of his power" (2 Thessalonians 1:8–9).

Faith in Christ does not make believers lawless; nay, the apostle speaks with some vehemence, "Do we then make void the law through faith? God forbid: yea, we establish the law" (Romans 3:31). Indeed, we are not under the law, that is, under the curse of the law, if we are true believers; nor are we under it as a covenant: "Do this and live." We are not to hope for justification by the law, nor to fear condemnation by it. But the law is a rule according to which we are bound to act and walk; and unto this rule our hearts and lives, with great care and conscience, should be conformed. And that these laws may be the better observed, the Lord and Lawgiver must be more eyed. He takes notice whether we yield obedience, and is most ready to assist us to obey. And He should always be set before us as both our Observer and our Helper. Psalm 16:8: "I have set the LORD always before me: because he is at my right hand, I shall not be moved."

6. God is Lord, who has power to save and to destroy. James 4:12: "There is one law-giver, who is able to save and to destroy: who art thou that judgest another?" He has the power of life and death; death that is eternal, life that is everlasting. He is the Lord of hosts; all creatures are at His command and beck, and are ready either to be the executioners of His wrath or to serve Him in His gracious purposes and pleasure. He is that mighty God who lifts up His hand to heaven and says, "I kill, and I make alive; I wound, and I heal: neither is there any that can deliver out of my hand. For I lift up my hand to heaven, and say, I live for ever" (Deuteronomy 32:39–40).

All sorts of life are from God, that of nature, grace, and glory. He can raise those who attend upon Him from the brink of the grave, and rescue them out of the very jaws of death. Psalm 30:2–3: "O LORD my God, I cried unto thee, and thou hast healed me. O LORD, thou hast brought up my soul from the grave: thou hast kept me alive, that I should not go down to the pit." Second Corinthians 1:9–10: "We had the sentence of death in ourselves, that we should not trust in ourselves, but in God which raiseth the dead: who delivered us from so great a death, and doth deliver: in whom we trust that he will yet deliver us." God is He who quickens, and makes those spiritually alive who were dead in sins and trespasses. He reverses the sentence of death that the law had passed upon them, gives them a new life and nature, and enables them to walk in newness of life. 'Tis a mighty voice, attended with His powerful Spirit, which raises those dead in sin and makes them live to God. John 5:25: "Verily, verily, I say unto you, The hour is coming, and now is, when the dead shall hear the voice of the Son of God: and they that hear shall live." And when this spiritual life is wrought, it brings eternal life in the seed and blossom, and into eternal life at length it shall be ripened and perfected. The sanctifying grace of the Spirit is likened unto water because it is of a cleansing, refreshing, and fructifying nature; and this grace shall still be acting and increasing till it issues in glory. John 4:14: "But the water that I shall give him shall be in him a well of water springing up into everlasting life."

And as all sorts of life are from God, so He has power to inflict all sorts of death. All afflictions and plagues, when this Lord sends them, say, "Here we are." The king of terrors, death, is God's subject, and says, "I am ready to strike young or old, high or low, few or many, as the Lord of all gives me commission and command." And the second death, at God's righteous pleasure, opens its everlasting doors to receive and eternally swallow up all whom He sentences there. Isaiah 5:14: "Therefore hell hath enlarged herself, and opened her mouth without measure: and their glory, and their multitude, and their pomp, and he that rejoiceth, shall descend into it." Such a Lord—the effects of whose love and anger are felt not only in this world, but also in the other, and indeed run parallel with eternity—should certainly be attended on with a great dread of offending Him, with the most exact care to please Him in everything.

7. God is a Lord obeyed by the whole creation except for men on earth, and for devils and damned spirits in hell. These greater lights, the sun and moon, that rule the day and night, are perfectly ruled by their Maker, and rise and set at His command. And to show that He can stop the sun in its swift motion, at Joshua's entreaty He commanded it to stand still in Gibeon, and the moon in the valley of Ajalon (Joshua 10:12). Nay, in the days of Hezekiah, He made the sun move backward no less than ten degrees from where it had gone down (Isaiah

38:8). All the stars of heaven He calls by their names, and they observe their courses according to His ordinances. The sea ebbs and flows according to His appointment, and keeps within the bounds that He has set for it when it roars and is most tempestuous. The storms and winds fulfill His Word, and if He does but say to them, "Peace, be still," presently there is a great calm. He calls the thunder and the lightning, and how terrible is the voice of the one and the flashing of the other! The thunder is silenced and the lightning extinguished at His pleasure. All creatures that glide through the air or slide through the ocean, that feed and grow upon the earth, in their way and manner obey their Maker and Preserver's will. Fie, oh, fie upon apostate angels and men, that they should be the only rebels! Look upward, downward, on the right hand, and on the left, and the many thousands of creatures that your eyes behold are so many instances of obedience to God. Why, oh, why should we not all be ready to yield our utmost service?

8. God is a Lord who overrules those who rebel against Him. Though they break His commands they cannot get from under His power. He can check, restrain, disappoint, and destroy them at His pleasure. The seed of the woman has been hated by the serpent's brood, and they who have been born only after the flesh have been strongly inclined to persecute such as have been born after the Spirit. Galatians 4:28–29: "Now we, brethren, as Isaac was, are the children of promise. But as then he that was born after the flesh persecuted him that was born after the Spirit, even so it is now." And so it is likely to be still. When heathen emperors and kings converted to the Christian faith, the prince of darkness did not turn and change. He always was, is, and will be full of malice against Christ the Head, and against His true members. And those who are of their father the devil, the lusts of their father they will do; and they who

are saints must expect to find those people's hearts set against them, and, as far as they can, their hands too.

But that Lord who is with His people is infinitely greater than the evil one. 1 John 4:4: "Ye are of God, little children, and have overcome them: because greater is he that is in you, than he that is in the world." As Satan's subtlety is nothing compared to God's wisdom, as his power is small to God's almightiness, so his wrath, though never so great, is a little and contemptible thing when the love that God bears to His people is believingly considered. The mightiest men whom Satan employs to run down the church of the living God shall never effect their wicked purpose; the church triumphs over her most furious enemies, looking unto her mighty Helper. Psalm 46:5–7: "God is in the midst of her; she shall not be moved: God shall help her, and that right early. The heathen raged, the kingdoms were moved." They stirred themselves up with their united force, and in their rage they would have devoured the Israel of God; but "He uttered his voice, and the earth melted." All these enemies were dispirited and came to nothing, and no wonder, for it follows: "The LORD of hosts is with us; the God of Jacob is our refuge." Well may the voluntary subjects of such a Lord attend upon Him with forwardness and faith, since He has such an absolute, uncontrollable dominion over all His and their enemies!

9. God is a Lord infinitely above and better than any other lords whatsoever. As He is infinitely superior to all in majesty and greatness, so also in mercy and goodness. The whole earth is full of divine goodness. Psalm 145:9: "The LORD is good to all: and his tender mercies are over all his works." It is special and peculiar kindness that is shown to His saints. Psalm 103:11: "As the heaven is high above the earth, so great is his mercy towards them that fear him." What are other lords if compared

with God? As for mammon, who has most of mankind to be his vassals, his delights are low, his riches uncertain, his all is vanity. Satan is a cruel lord; he is a liar who deceives, a murderer who destroys all whom he can keep under his power and dominion. And the wages that sin gives to them who serve it is eternal death; and the more diligent they have been in the service of sin, and the more laborious workers of iniquity, their hell will be so much the hotter, their sorrow and misery so much the greater.

Are such lords as these comparable to the Lord Jehovah, whose strength, whose love is everlasting? What care does He take of all who are truly His servants! How mild and gentle is His government! His kingdom is righteousness, peace, and joy. It was a pious spontaneous prayer of Augustine: "O Lord, give that which Thou commandest." His servants are by Himself created in Christ Jesus unto the good works in which He has commanded them to walk. He teaches them by His own Spirit to do His will. Psalm 143:10: "Teach me to do thy will; for thou art my God: thy spirit is good; lead me into the land of uprightness." He works in them to will, inclining their hearts unto His testimonies; and He works in them to do His own good pleasure (Philippians 2:13). He directs their ways to keep His statutes. All the good that good men do, God is the Doer. His preventing and assisting grace is and does all in all. And after all, He crowns that grace which He Himself has wrought and made active with an eternal weight of glory. Well may His attendants glory in such a Lord, who is peerless! Psalm 34:2–3: "My soul shall make her boast in the LORD: the humble shall hear thereof, and be glad. O magnify the LORD with me, and let us exalt his name together."

10. God is the Lord and Judge of all, at whose bar angels and men, the quick and the dead, must at last stand. Apostate

angels believe and tremble at the foresight of future judgment. Satan's time is short and his wrath great; but his dread is greater of that great day of reckoning and retribution. And as for the children of men, all must be judged; the day is appointed and is hastening. Every one of us, said the apostle, must give account of himself to God (Romans 14:12). And an account will be taken of all that has been done while we were in the body. Ecclesiastes 12:14: "For God shall bring every work into judgment, with every secret thing, whether it be good, or whether it be evil." How should this Lord and Judge be feared! With what diligence should His commandments be kept, since this is the whole existence of man! Man's duty, safety, grand concern, and interest lie here. He who will judge all at last with His own eyes observes and sees all at present. Psalm 11:4: "The LORD's throne is in heaven: his eyes behold, his eyelids try, the children of men." Job 31:4: "Doth not he see my ways, and count all my steps?" And when all the children of men who ever were or shall be appear before Him, He will own His faithful attendants and put great honor upon them. And then He will say, "Well done, good and faithful servants. You have been faithful in a few things. I will make you rulers over many things. Enter into the joy of your Lord." But how shall the children of disobedience stand before Him, who lived and died in their rebellion and wickedness, and have done nothing but treasure up wrath against the day of wrath, and against the revelation of the righteous judgment of God?

CHAPTER 9

How God's Lordship Should Impact Our Attending upon Him

Second, I am to manifest what influence and effect the apprehension of God's being the Lord should have upon us when we attend upon Him.

1. When we look upon God as Lord, we should be sensible of our distance, and how we are infinitely below Him. What a sense was there of the divine majesty, and of his own meanness, in the patriarch Abraham when he spoke those words in Genesis 18:27: "Behold now, I have taken upon me to speak unto the Lord, which am but dust and ashes." We read that dominion and fear are with Him, that the brightest stars are not pure in His sight; "how much less man, that is a worm? and the son of man, which is a worm?" (Job 25:2, 5–6). The grace of the gospel does not exclude a holy awe and reverence of God, but includes it. And the more there is of grace, the more there is also of this godly fear, and the service is the more acceptable. Hebrews 12:28–29: "Wherefore we receiving a kingdom which cannot be moved, let us have grace, whereby we may serve God acceptably with reverence and godly fear: for our God is a consuming fire." We are indeed encouraged to come with boldness, but that boldness is upon the account of our great High Priest and Mediator. But though we are the members

of Christ, we must remember that God is inconceivably above us. The man Christ Jesus Himself, when He prayed, fell on His face before His heavenly Father (Matthew 26:39). Nay, He calls Himself a worm too in Psalm 22:6: "But I am a worm, and no man; a reproach of men, and despised of the people."

2. When we look upon God as Lord, we should be deeply humbled and abased for our affronts, offenses, and rebellions against Him. 'Tis the law of the Lord Almighty that sin breaks; and 'tis the Lord Himself whom sin causes to be despised. When David was truly penitent and contrite, he cried out, "Against thee, thee only have I sinned, and done this evil in thy sight" (Psalm 51:4). His sin had been an injury, and indeed a deadly one, to Uriah his subject; but it was a gross and foul breach of the law of God, and so was committed against Him. And as his sin was ever before him, so was that Lord against whom he had sinned. This laid him very low, and made him ready to condemn himself and to justify God, however severe a sentence should be passed; however sore a punishment should be inflicted upon him: "That thou mightest be justified when thou speakest, and be clear when thou judgest."

Job had not been so careful of God's honor as he had been to vindicate his own innocence. At length the Lord Himself manifested His glory to him. He confounded him with that question in Job 40:8, "Wilt thou also disannul my judgment? wilt thou condemn me, that thou mayest be righteous?" Job at length had a clearer view of the greatness and sovereignty of that God with whom he had to do and said, "I have heard of thee by the hearing of the ear: but now mine eye seeth thee. Wherefore I abhor myself, and repent in dust and ashes" (Job 42:5–6).

3. When we look upon God as Lord, we should admire His concern for the salvation and happiness of such as we are. An eminent saint and a great king stated, "O my soul, thou hast

said unto the LORD, Thou art my Lord: my goodness extendeth not to thee" (Psalm 16:2). He is a Lord so high, so glorious in Himself, so far exalted above all, that the goodness of the best cannot in the least degree be beneficial to Him. He does not stand in need of man; therefore the goodwill that He bears toward men is the more to be admired. If the whole human race, after the first defection from God, had perished, and every one of them had been miserable forever, the blessedness of God would have been no more impaired than it was by the loss and misery of those spirits that first sinned and left their own habitation—none of which ever was recovered or shall be. Oh, why is it that the Lord of glory should show such discriminating grace to the sons of men! Lord, what is man that Thou, who art so much above him, should be so mindful of him as to visit him with Thy salvation, who was unable to save himself, unworthy to be saved, nay, unwilling to be saved, till Thou didst make him willing in the day of Thy power?

4. When we look upon God as Lord, we should exceedingly dread His wrath and value His loving-kindness. The rebukes of such a mighty Lord, when provoked, must be terrible. Psalm 18:7: "Then the earth shook and trembled; the foundations also of the hills moved and were shaken, because he was wroth." Exodus 15:6–7: "Thy right hand, O LORD, is become glorious in power: Thy right hand, O LORD, hath dashed in pieces the enemy. And in the greatness of thine excellency thou hast overthrown them that rose up against thee: thou sentest forth thy wrath, which consumed them as stubble." And as the anger of God has all evils in its power to inflict on those who are so foolhardy as to provoke it, so His loving-kindness is ready to open the treasures of His goodness. How bountiful is His love for His beloved ones! The psalmist, having meditated on it, justly stood amazed at it and cried out, "How excellent

is thy loving-kindness, O God!" (Psalm 36:7). It transcends all created love; if all the love that is in men and angels were united together, it would not be so much, compared with the love of God, as the light of a glowworm is to the sun, shining forth in its noonday glory. And as the love of God is so excellent in itself, transcendently excellent also are the acts and beneficial effects of it.

If the wrath of a king is as the messengers of death (Proverbs 16:14), what is the wrath of the King of kings and Lord of lords! If in the light of the king's countenance is life, and his favor is as the cloud of the latter rain (Proverbs 16:15), the favor of the blessed and only Potentate must be infinitely more refreshing and better than life itself. It is from this Lord that every man's judgment comes. He ministers judgment at present; good and evil are dispensed by His hand, and 'tis He who will pass upon all the final sentence of absolution or condemnation at the last day. What care then should there be to have His wrath appeased by a Mediator! What fervency of spirit should sue for peace and reconciliation! Solomon tells us that many seek the ruler's favor; but certainly divine favor is much more desirable because every man's judgment is from the Lord (Proverbs 29:26).

5. When we look upon God as Lord, we should trust in Him for deliverance from other lords who have had the dominion over us. He can work whatsoever and in whomsoever He pleases, and none shall be able to hinder. The psalmist was sensible of sin's force and power; he was weary of sin's dominion and cried unto God to deliver him from the reign of all the sins he knew; and as for those sins that were secret and concealed from his view, he begs that he might be convinced of them, and thoroughly cleansed from them (Psalm 19:12–13). The Lord can turn the heart perfectly to hate the sin that was most

of all beloved; and the strength of sin is gone once it is hated. And as the hatred grows stronger and stronger, sin becomes weaker and weaker daily. Saul was a proud, self-confident Pharisee, a furious persecutor; the Lord met him and stopped him in his persecuting rage. He humbled him and worked in his heart faith in Christ, against whom he had such a mighty and seemingly invincible prejudice. From a wolf, He turned him into one of the sheep of Christ, nay, into a zealous and careful shepherd of the flock, so that he preached that faith which he once endeavored to destroy (Galatians 1:23).

The Lord can subdue iniquity where it has held the greatest sway. If He speaks the word of power, down go all strongholds; reasonings that before were thought to be strong are seen to be absurd. Vain imaginations, high things and thoughts, are brought into captivity and obedience. 2 Corinthians 10:4–5: "For the weapons of our warfare are not carnal, but mighty through God to the pulling down of strong holds; casting down imaginations, and every high thing that exalteth itself against the knowledge of God, and bringing into captivity every thought to the obedience of Christ."

The very prince of the devils, Beelzebub himself, the Lord can easily dispossess. He cast him out of heaven, and surely He can cast him out of the heart also. If the Lord speaks the word, Satan falls like lightning—and how sudden and remarkable is his downfall! If He charges this unclean spirit to come out, he must immediately leave his habitation; and if He commands him to keep out, he must enter no more. Mark 9:25: "He rebuked the foul spirit, saying unto him, Thou dumb and deaf spirit, I charge thee, come out of him, and enter no more into him."

When the Lord, by the preaching of the gospel, made Himself known in the world, how were heathen idols destroyed! First Thessalonians 1:9: "Ye turned to God from idols, to serve the living and true God." And whatever worldly enjoyments have been idolized, He can show the vanity of them, and mortify inordinate affection for them. He is jealous of His honor, and does not like to have His throne usurped. We are to trust in this Lord, and to desire that He would take His great power and reign in us, and that no opposite lords may be any longer served.

6. When we look upon God as Lord, we should be careful to know His will, and always forward to do it. That is one of the first inquiries of a true convert: "Lord, what wilt Thou have me to do?" Man's will, till renewed by grace, is foolish, perverse, wicked, and perniciously inclined. He wills that which is to His own woe. 'Tis but reasonable that such a will should yield to the will of God who is wise, holy, and good. Whoever acted according to the will of God and saw cause to repent of it? And sure I am that they who do contrary to the will of God must repent of it in this world, for it will be too late in the next one. We find that wisdom is very much placed in knowing the will of God. Ephesians 5:17: "Wherefore be ye not unwise, but understanding what the will of the Lord is." And happiness is placed in doing it in John 13:17: "If ye know these things, happy are ye if ye do them." We should approve ourselves as better servants if we did but mind more our Lord and Master's will. In temptation we should consider what is the will of God, and then the tempter would be withstood. When earthly treasure is laid before us to draw our hearts to covet it, we should remember that it is the will of the Lord that our heart and treasure should be in heaven. Whatever duty we are setting about, whether towards God or man, we should inquire how God would have this duty be done. What acceptable service then would God have from us! And what blessings should we be to those whom we are related to and converse with! "Lord, show me Thy will, and let my will, in all things and at all times, be determined by Thine!" This is

becoming language, and every soul should sincerely speak it. He is the most eminent and perfect Christian who stands most perfect and complete in all the will of God.

7. When we look upon God as Lord, we should never quarrel or murmur at anything He is pleased to do to us or with us. Arbitrary power is very much affected by the potentates of this world, though it would be much more truly great in them to do as they ought than to do as they please. Arbitrary power is justly claimed by the Lord, the universal Sovereign. He may do whatever He pleases; and it will please Him to do nothing but what becomes His own wisdom, goodness, and other glorious excellencies. A mighty monarch who had walked in pride at length was so abased that he acknowledged and honored this highest Lord of all, saying, "All the inhabitants of the earth are reputed as nothing: and he doeth according to his will in the army of heaven, and among the inhabitants of the earth" (Daniel 4:35). The dispensations of divine providence must not fall under our censure. He who reproves God will answer ill for it. 'Tis sinful boldness to strive with Him and say, "What doest Thou?" as if He had not done as well as He might have. 'Tis more becoming, with obedient patience and submission, to cry out, "O the depth of the riches both of the wisdom and knowledge of God! how unsearchable are his judgments, and his ways past finding out!" (Romans 11:33). And Psalm 145:17: "The LORD is righteous in all his ways, and holy in all his works." When under His severe dealings with us we charge Him with rigor and want of care, we do but charge God foolishly. His understanding is infinite (Psalm 147:5); therefore He is not liable to the least mistake. His compassions are tender, and He can never become cruel. 'Tis inconsistent with His justice to lay upon any man more than is right, that he should enter into judgment with God (Job 34:23). He is so gracious that He

afflicts when His people need to be afflicted, and thus it is good for them to be afflicted. That man spoke very ill who said, "I do well to be angry." Whatever the Lord does to His people, He does wisely, justly, and faithfully; how then can their fretting and impatience be justified! It would be far better for them to cease their contention and disputing, and to answer as Job at last did in Job 40:4–5, "Behold, I am vile; what shall I answer thee? I will lay mine hand upon my mouth. Once have I spoken; but I will not answer: yea, twice; but I will proceed no further."

8. When we look upon God as Lord, we should long to behold His glory in His kingdom. It was the desire of Moses in Exodus 33:18, "I beseech thee, shew me thy glory." The saints see but little of the King in comparison to what they shall see. They know but in part, and how should they long that that which is perfect may come, and that which is in part may be done away (1 Corinthians 13:10). The earth is the Lord's footstool, and here we behold but some footsteps and shadows, and have a darker discovery of Him. But heaven is His throne, and when we come to stand before His throne, how bright will His majesty be in our eyes! How glorious His holiness! How will His face be all light and love! And how ravishing will the fullest sense of that love be! It should be our care, by a continual increase of purity in heart, to be fitted for this beatific vision of the Lord of glory. Matthew 5:8: "Blessed are the pure in heart: for they shall see God." And this vision should be the more longed for because it will be transforming. When we behold the Lord's glory, we shall partake of it. When we see Him, we shall, to our eternal excellence and satisfaction, be like Him. 1 John 3:2: "Beloved, now are we the sons of God, and it doth not yet appear what we shall be: but we know that, when he shall appear, we shall be like him; for we shall see him as he is."

CHAPTER 10

Reproofs and Advice for Those Who Don't Attend upon God as Lord

USE OF REPROOF. Well may the mouth of His messengers be full of reproof, since the Lord who sent them is so generally disregarded. Several sorts of persons are worthy of reprehension.

1. They are to be reproved who say with Pharaoh, "Who is the Lord that we should obey his voice?" How many are there who will not acknowledge that they owe Him any service; or, if they do acknowledge it, they are so wicked and unrighteous that they will not render what they cannot but confess is due to Him! How many say, "Our lips are our own: who is lord over us?" (Psalm 12:4). Who is He, they ask, who would give laws to our tongues, and put them under a bridle? They say also, "Our members are all our own, and therefore we will employ them as we please [though that employing is abusing and abasing them to be instruments of unrighteousness unto sin]. Our time also is our own, and therefore we will pass it according to our own pleasure"—as if time were a thing of no value, and to have it well or ill with them to eternity were a matter of mere indifference. They who now cry, "Who is the Lord?" will stand, as they all must, before His judgment seat, and then He will make them know who He is. How terrifying will His looks be! How

heavy will His hand be felt! They would not obey the scepter of His Word, and He will "break them with a rod of iron; and dash them in pieces like a potter's vessel" (Psalm 2:9).

2. They are to be reproved who have a greater reverence for man than for God, who is the sovereign Lord of all. They dare not displease great men, but the great God they are bold to offend. Men whom they depend upon, they are careful to stay on good terms with; but that God in whose hand their breath is, and whose are all their ways, they do not glorify. They depend upon this Lord for their being and blessedness, and for all things. Their life is continued only during His pleasure; all things that they have are of His bestowing, and if ever they are blessed it is God who must make them so. And yet the favor and anger of this God are condemned in comparison to the love and hatred of man. How many will comply with the lusts of men who will not conform to the will of God? Men's inventions are regarded more than God's institutions. Thus "the statutes of Omri were kept, and all the works of the house of Ahab, and Israel did walk in their counsels" (Micah 6:16), when they rejected the counsel of God against themselves and cast the laws of Jehovah behind their backs. But how poor a thing is man's help against divine anger! Nay, here the mightiest man can be no security. Job 9:13: "If God will not withdraw his anger, the proud helpers do stoop under him." And those whom the Lord undertakes to comfort, why should men who shall die dismay them? Isaiah 51:12–13: "I, even I, am he that comforteth you: who art thou, that thou shouldest be afraid of a man that shall die, and of the son of man which shall be made as grass; and forgettest the LORD thy maker, that hath stretched forth the heavens, and laid the foundations of the earth?" His power may well make the fury of oppressors

contemptible. But God's power is as irresistible as His wrath is intolerable.

3. *They are to be reproved who prefer the worst lords before the greatest and the best Lord of all.* The true God is certainly the best Lord, and sin and Satan are the worst that can be served—and yet how few the former has, and how many servants does the latter have! The Lord's government is most gracious; the paths He requires us to walk in are pleasantness and peace. But the ways of sin are quite contrary. "No peace, saith my God, to the wicked" (Isaiah 57:21). Whatever sin in the beginning may seem, its end is bitter as wormwood, sharp as a two-edged sword; and they who serve it, their feet go down to death, and their steps will quickly take hold of hell.

Shall I show you the manner of sin and Satan's reign? Their vassals are put upon cruel, hard service, and they must halt at nothing. If the fulfilling of their lusts calls for it, the estate must be wasted, health must be endangered, repute and good name must be disregarded, posterity must be beggared, life itself must be shortened, and the precious soul lost forever rather than sin not be gratified and served. Sin has a law, and what command does it impose upon those who are subject to it? Its injunctions are such as these: "Fight against God, and slight the wrath of the Lord Almighty; mind neither your duty nor your safety; pursue vanity and vexation of spirit, but do not care for the truest and eternal blessedness; be sure to please your flesh and seek yourself and mind your carnal interest, though you are in the worst sense undone thereby. Go on impenitently and securely in your wickedness, till you fall into the flames of hell. Do all this and die, and damn yourself to eternity." What hard sayings are these! Yet thousands and millions hear and obey them! It is amazing that those who have reasonable souls should act so devoid of all sound reason as to refuse His service, who commands them to be wise, safe, and good, and should choose to be fools and to be miserable!

4. They are to be reproved who have begun to serve the Lord, and afterwards forsake His service and revolt from Him. These revolters show a great zeal and forwardness in religion, many of them, for a time; they seem to have escaped the pollutions of the world, to have gotten the victory over it, and to have overcome the evil one. But being again entangled and overcome by mammon and Satan, they are a credit to these masters, and to their false and pernicious ways—but they are a great dishonor to religion, and to the Author of it, the Lord of glory. These revolters discover an evil heart of unbelief in departing from the living God, which is so much cautioned against in Hebrews 3:12; and if without faith it is impossible to please God, how much must He be provoked by infidelity! And with what torments will their unbelief at last be confuted and punished together! These revolters quench a great deal of light which has shone into them, so as to aggravate the works of darkness unto which they return. Though under conviction they have felt the terrors of the Lord, yet they venture more than ever to incense Him; in a special manner they grieve the Spirit of God and deeply wound their own spirits. But these wounds are not felt at present because their consciences are seared. Satan has fuller and faster possession of them; fullness of sin quickly follows; and the last state with them is worse than the first.

USE OF ADVICE

1. Hearken to the Lord inviting and calling you all to His service. There is room in His house for many thousands more than are there, and there is plentiful and abundant provision for their entertainment. "In my father's house," said the prod-

igal when he came to himself, "there is bread enough and to spare" (Luke 15:17). Christ's sacrifice of Himself can put away multitudes of sins more than as yet have been pardoned. And though millions of empty and lost souls more come to Him, out of His fullness they may all be replenished, and made secure under the shadow of His wings. His messengers say to you, "Come." He Himself says, "Come." His Spirit says, "Come." Your wants, which none but He can supply, speak aloud to you to go to Him. Keep therefore no longer at a distance. He is most ready to receive you graciously, and to communicate grace of all sorts to you.

2. Behold how willing this Lord is to pass by all past disobedience upon your believing and repenting. The Apostle Paul was not upbraided with his persecuting rage and hellish fury when he submitted himself to the Lord and laid down the weapons wherewith he had fought against God. "The grace of our Lord was exceeding abundant with faith and love which is in Christ Jesus" (1 Timothy 1:14). And in verses 15–16 he tells us that he, the chief of sinners, obtained mercy that the greatest sinners hereafter may hope and expect mercy upon their believing and conversion: "Howbeit for this cause I obtained mercy, that in me first Jesus Christ might shew forth all longsuffering, for a pattern to them which should hereafter believe on him to life everlasting." Whatever your rebellions have been, if now you are willing and obedient, all shall be forgotten and forgiven. Scarlet and crimson sins shall become white as snow and wool (Isaiah 1:18–19).

3. See where your righteousness and strength lie. Jesus Christ the righteous is the righteousness of them who believe. His obedience and sufferings can satisfy for and cover all your disobedience, and 'tis through Him alone that you attain the

free gift of justification of life. He became obedient to death, even the death of the cross; and 'tis by the obedience of this one, the second Adam, that as many as believe in Him are made righteous. And as in the Lord you have righteousness, so in Him you have strength too. His power must rest upon you, or else no good will be done by you. Through His strength all things may be done, but He Himself says, "Without me ye can do nothing" (John 15:5). Never think by good works to satisfy for bad ones. The best works have much amiss in them. And by no means entertain an imagination that at your own pleasure you can work in yourselves to will and to do; but always acknowledge the necessity and efficacy of the grace of Christ, and glorify that grace, saying, when you obey and labor, "It is not I, but the grace of God that is with me."

4. Earnestly desire that your hearts may be circumcised to love both the Lord Himself and His service likewise. It is a promise worth more, and if made good to us will enrich us more, than the wealth of both the Indies. Deuteronomy 30:6: "The LORD thy God will circumcise thine heart, and the heart of thy seed, to love the LORD thy God with all thine heart, and with all thy soul, that thou mayest live." A heart to love Him is His own gift, and the heart must be circumcised by Him before it will be brought to love Him. The prophet speaks of the foreskin of the heart that must be taken away. Now this foreskin of the heart is carnal and worldly love, together with enmity against God and His law. Cry to the Lord according to His good word of promise to mortify the one and to subdue the other, and that He would give you a new heart and nature, cause a new light to shine that may manifest His glorious goodness in the face of Christ, and so direct your hearts into the love of Himself. If He is truly loved, He will be the more willingly obeyed; and truly His precepts are worthy to be loved too.

The better they are kept, the more truly excellent are those who keep them, and they are kept in more perfect peace. The psalmist said, "My soul hath kept thy testimonies; and I love them exceedingly" (Psalm 119:167). And no wonder, for he had said before in verse 165, "Great peace have they which love thy law: and nothing shall offend them." Such a Lord, such a law deserves love, and love will sweeten service; it will not count this service as tedious, but will mightily incline the heart to perseverance in its duty.

5. Let your fear and awe of the Lord's majesty, when you attend upon Him, be joined with a hope in His mercy. If fear and hope are thus joined together, as you will be the more encouraged in God, so God will take the more pleasure in you. For "the Lord taketh pleasure in them that fear him, in those that hope in his mercy" (Psalm 147:11). The mercy of God is magnified in His Word on purpose so that hope may be raised, and rise still higher and higher. This Lord on whom you ought to attend is rich in mercy. His merciful kindness is great. He has mercy, not upon the account of merit in man, but because He will have mercy (Romans 9:18). And how often is it said in Psalm 136 that "His mercy endureth forever." Here is a large and firm foundation for hope to build on. And if your hope is not presumptuous, but of a purifying nature, you may, from such a merciful Lord, confidently expect that grace and those good things you need in time. And when your short time is at an end, the best things of all remain unto eternity.

PART THREE

Attending upon God Should Be without Distraction

CHAPTER 11

How the Heart Is Distracted

DOCTRINE 3: Attendance upon God should be without distraction. 'Tis not only apostasy from the faith and the practice of religion which the apostle bids us to take heed of—which is a more gross departing away from God—but he cautions against any withdrawings of heart from that Lord with whom we have to do. Therefore, in a time of distress and persecution, he prefers a single state before wedlock; not that marriage considered in itself has anything of sin in it, for 'tis honorable in all ways, and it is not that a single state in itself has anything of holiness, but because the cares that attend marriage are apt to distract the mind and hinder the things that belong to the Lord from being cared for as they ought and might be. Indeed, the context plainly intimates that it is a great part of Christian prudence to so order our secular affairs, and to choose such a condition of life, as may be most subservient to our spiritual designs, and may least interfere with our main business, which is the Lord's service, that it may be done without distraction. They are pronounced to be the blessed ones who keep God's testimonies, and who seek Him with their whole heart (Psalm 119:2). And since the whole heart must seek Him, the thoughts, the affections, and all of the heart must attend upon Him; nothing of the soul must be absent or withdrawn. The prophet speaks of the heart's engaging to approach unto God in Jeremiah 30:21: "For who is this that engaged his heart to approach unto me? saith the LORD." That the heart may be thus engaged for God, it must be disengaged from other things, and all that is within it too must be engaged to approach Him. When Moses and the children of Israel were to go into the wilderness to serve the Lord, they went with their young and old, with their flocks and their herds, there was not a hoof left behind (Exodus 10:26). And when we go to serve our God, we should go with our all. No power of our souls should be exempted; not so much as a thought should be left behind.

In handling this doctrine I shall:

First, tell you what distraction in attending upon God is.

Second, tell you what it is to attend upon the Lord without distraction.

Third, assign the reasons why we should take heed of distraction in serving Him with such care.

Fourth, in the next chapter, deal with some cases of conscience about these distractions.

Fifth, in the final chapter, make application.

First, I am to tell you what distraction in attending upon God is. 'Tis the first step toward a cure to know our disease and to have a right sense of it. Several things are here to be premised:

1. **Distraction is the fault of the heart.** That deceitful and wicked thing, how many faults it has! And how often does it withdraw when we have to do with God, flying as Jonah from His presence, and being anywhere but where it should be! Indeed, sometimes this distraction too visibly and scandalously appears by unnecessary whisperings, by salutations when persons are in God's sanctuary and service, by the wandering of the eye,

and by other irreverent carriage and behavior in the time of worship. These, when ordinarily allowed, are plain indications that the heart is not in God's work and, which is worse, does not care to be engaged therein. And how blameworthy then it is! It is the heart which foolishly departs from the Lord. It is not so right and steadfast with Him as it should be. Psalm 78:8: "A generation that set not their heart aright, and whose spirit was not stedfast with God" has a brand set upon them so that we may take heed of being like them.

2. Distraction is a fault that is most easily incurred. As the leaves of some trees waver with the least stirring of the wind, so the mind of man is apt to waver and discover its natural instability when corruption stirs within or Satan endeavors to put the heart into disorder. How far may the heart, if it is not strictly watched, wander all of a sudden, as far as the east is from the west, nay, as far as earth is from heaven! 'Tis natural for the soul to lift itself up to vanity. This is intimated plainly by the psalmist when he describes the acceptable attendant on God to be one who has not lifted up his soul to vanity (Psalm 24:4). By "vanity" we may understand idols that are called by that name, or the vanities of the world, which the heart is so prone to gad and rove after, even when duties of the greatest importance are being performed, that ought to be performed with the greatest fixedness of thoughts and seriousness imaginable.

3. The longer the distraction is, the worse it is. A heart which is truly good and honest may be seized on by distraction before it is aware. The evil one may step into the chariot and begin to drive it away from God; deceitful sin may suddenly arise in the soul and begin to disturb and defile it. But when this is quickly observed, and the wakeful conscience checks the heart—and when the upright heart is glad for the admonition, presently

checks itself, and immediately returns to its Lord and to its work and duty—Satan misses his aim, and the duty shall not be lost. The soul that follows hardest after God may sometimes stumble; but if as soon as it is down it is up again and runs the faster, this running will not be in vain.

But when distraction continues for a great while, it argues that the conscience is not so vigilant and faithful as it should be, in that it does not correct these vagrant thoughts that come into the mind. There is a fault also in the heart that it can so patiently endure such vain guests to lodge in it for so long a time before they are turned out of doors. The psalmist says that his spirit made diligent search (Psalm 77:6). A spirit that does so will quickly take notice of these roving imaginations, and will endeavor to thrust them out as soon as they are found. But if there is a carelessness, and too great a connivance at these wanderings, though the soul may not be quite dead in sin, yet there is much of a spiritual lethargy and sleepiness, which is the image of spiritual death.

4. If distractions in holy duties are ordinarily allowed, they argue the heart not to be right with God. When the heart is constantly absent from ordinances, and does not care to be better inclined and disposed to them; when it willingly is at mammon's and Satan's command, even when the body draws nigh to God, and there is lip honor and lip service given to Him—this argues plainly that the heart is unrenewed, and remains alienated and estranged from the Lord. The heart must still be carnal and wicked, and at enmity against God, that is like the eyes of fools in the end of the earth (Proverbs 17:24), when things above should be sought, and heaven should be minded.

These things being premised, I shall tell you what distraction in attending upon God is in the following particulars.

PARTICULAR 1. The heart is distracted in this attendance when its thoughts are impertinent and vain. These kinds of thoughts may well be called "legion," for they are many. They are like the motes in the sun or the bubbles in the water on a rainy day, innumerable. These thoughts hover about the minds of the best when they engage in holy duties, and will presently intrude if they are not kept out with a very strict guard. But where they are entertained, they draw off the heart from the work at hand, and the Lord sees it and is displeased. Psalm 94:11: "The LORD knoweth the thoughts of man, that they are vanity," and impertinence is not the smallest part of this vanity. Vain man is compared to a wild ass's colt in Job 11:12. The silliness of that creature, and its frisks and motions to little purpose, are a fit representation of the mind of man, and of its foolish sallies and vagaries in the Lord's service. Who does not have reason to cry out with the psalmist in Psalm 69:5: "O God, thou knowest my foolishness; and my sins are not hid from thee"? If in the performance of holy duties the tongue should fall to talking of some other matter, and idle and vain discourse should proceed out of the lips, this would be a scandalous distraction that others might take notice of. Now thinking is the mind's speaking, and the Heart-searcher can and does more easily take notice when the mind thinks impertinently than we can observe when the tongue speaks so.

PARTICULAR 2. The heart is distracted when in religious duties its thoughts are wicked and vile. Our Lord, who well knew what was in man, tells us in Matthew 15:19, "Out of the heart proceed evil thoughts." These are the first bad offspring, and the greatest wickedness that is acted begins with them. How great was man's wickedness upon the earth when "God saw that…every imagination of the thoughts of his heart was only evil continually" (Genesis 6:5). Now if thoughts are evil continually, they don't cease to be evil when duties of religion are engaged in. When proud thoughts, wanton and filthy thoughts, worldly thoughts, envious, malicious, and vengeful thoughts, or any other wicked imaginations have a place in the heart, these, as swarms of pesky flies, corrupt men's services and make their sacrifices unto God to become abominable. By these the mind not only wanders from God, but is alienated and estranged from Him. The heart is in hell while the eyes are looking up to heaven and the tongue is speaking to the God who dwells there. When a man with a heart full of such sinful thoughts approaches God, how loathsome must he be to His pure and piercing eye! The Lord beholds and knows him afar off (Psalm 138:6). And indeed, what fellowship can there be between holiness and pollution? It is much more unbecoming and dangerous for such a one to approach the presence of God than it would be for the foulest leper, with the nastiest garments, to come before the greatest emperor on the face of the earth.

PARTICULAR 3. The heart is distracted in attending on God when hellish injections are entertained. Satan shows his deep and inveterate enmity against God in these blasphemous injections, and he creates a very troublesome disturbance to us in the Lord's service; he has fiery darts whereby he endeavors to cause hellfire in our consciences by despairing agonies and horrors. And blasphemous thoughts are like fiery bombs that he shoots into our souls to put us into disorder in our duties, and utterly out of frame. Sometimes this wickedly bold, foul, and wretched spirit will give the vilest names to the blessed God, names that are given to the worst of men. Sometimes he will say that divine favor and fury are both contemptible, and, as if He were a mere idol, that it is not in Him to do good or to do evil (Zephaniah 1:12)—whereas, indeed, penal evils are all from Him. Amos 3:6: "Shall there be evil in a city, and the LORD hath not done it?" And the psalmist tells us in Psalm 33:5, "He loveth righteousness and judgment: the earth is full of the goodness of the LORD."

Sometimes Satan will deny the providence of God, and say, "How doth God know? And is there knowledge in the Most High?" It is as if He did not regard men or their ways, but rather as if all things in this world fall out either according to blind chance or fatal necessity. Whereas the psalmist, with great force and evidence of reason, argues in Psalm 94:9–10: "He that planted the ear, shall he not hear? he that formed the eye, shall he not see?...he that teacheth man knowledge, shall not he know?" Nay, sometimes this evil one, though he himself believes in God and trembles before Him, yet will inject atheistic thoughts, and confidently deny the very being of God so that he may discourage all religion and application to Him, whereas "the heavens declare the glory of God." As the light of the sun is evident, so it is evident there is a God, by whom that sun was made, and all things visible besides.

Finally, this lying spirit will attack with great violence and blasphemous falsehoods against the Word and gospel of Jesus Christ. Christ was manifested to destroy the works of the devil; thus the devil will endeavor to hinder the Word of Christ from being believed, though God Himself bore witness to the truth of this Word, both with signs and wonders, and with divers miracles and gifts of the Holy Ghost, according to His own will (Hebrews 2:4), and though miraculous operations of grace do not cease to this day. When a blind mind is made to see; when a heart of stone is turned into a heart of flesh; when the dead in sin are made alive to God; when righteousness is their practice and their conversation is in heaven—all this shows a divine efficacy in the Word, and its divine authority and most certain truth.

These hellish injections must by no means have an undisturbed abode in the mind; for if they do, they will cut the sinews of all religious endeavors. They will dampen the affections, deaden the heart, and eat away all manner of gracious inclinations and purposes. These blasphemous injections show that there is a devil, for even nature, as bad as it is, will rise against some of the vile thoughts he casts in. He is an enemy to God, to righteousness, to the souls of men, and as great a liar as he is an enemy; therefore he is not at all to be credited, but his wickedness and falsehoods are to be abhorred.

PARTICULAR 4. The heart is distracted when, though its thoughts are good, they are unseasonable. A good thought becomes a bad one when it is entertained at a time that is not proper for it. If when we are confessing sin, a thought, good in itself, but alien to the matter at hand, arises that draws the mind away from thinking of sin, and has no tendency to humble and break the heart for its sin, this thought, by its unseasonableness, becomes evil. If when we are petitioning for mercy, a good thought should intrude and make us forget what we are doing, and we neither mind what we are asking nor to whom we are speaking, a good thought in this case causes a sinful distraction. Solomon says that everything is beautiful in its time in Ecclesiastes 3:11: "A word spoken in due season, how good is it!" (Proverbs 15:23). And just like words, so thoughts are the better the more seasonable they are. If the subtle serpent cannot divert the mind from performing its duty by bad thoughts, he will endeavor to do it by good ones. If when hearing the Word preached we fall to reading the Scripture to ourselves, or our minds are upon a piece of a sermon that we heard at another time, and the truths propounded and the duties pressed are not at all regarded—alas, we are but too much like the stony ground, and the seed is caught away as soon as it is sown.

PARTICULAR 5. The heart is distracted when the mind and judgment are so carnal and perverted as to esteem earthly things above spiritual and eternal ones. When our Lord says, "The light of the body is the eye," in Matthew 6:22, He intimates that what the eye is to the body, the judgment is to the soul, and indeed to the whole man. If the judgment is rectified and apprehends things aright, the actings of the soul will be the better; but if the judgment is darkened and does not discern between truth and falsehood, between good and evil, between substance and shadows, the soul must wander away from God and lose itself quickly. When the judgment is perverted, there is a very wicked distraction of mind; for the judgment gives sentence against God and for the creature, as if a portion in this life were more worthy to be chosen and secured than an inheritance that is eternal. It was said to the rich man in hell, "Son, remember that thou in thy lifetime receivedst thy good things" (Luke 16:25). They are called his "good things" because his mistaking mind apprehended them to be good indeed, and the best things of all were not, in his judgment, so good as these. How can the natural man not be distracted in all the duties he performs to God, since his darkened mind thinks such duties unprofitable, and that the things of God are foolishness? First Corinthians 2:14: "The natural man receiveth not the things of the Spirit of God: for they are foolishness unto him: neither can he know them, because they are spiritually discerned."

PARTICULAR 6. The heart is distracted when the will and affections withdraw from God and fasten upon vanity. A false judgment being passed, no wonder that a foolish choice is made. This is an ill distraction indeed when the bias of the will turns away from God and refuses to be subject to Him, though He is the best Lord, and cares as little to enjoy Him as to obey Him. The Lord observed and complained of this in Psalm 81:11: "Israel would none of me." He offered no less than Himself to them, who is so infinitely desirable, who was so all-sufficient and able to fulfill their desires, in whom the truest delight was to be found, and yet this greatest and best offer was condemned. And when the heart and affections are thus denied to God, how are they bestowed? Pleasures are loved more than God, and even in His house; and when there is an external service yielded, "their heart goeth after their covetousness" (Ezekiel 33:31). There is a greediness after gain, no hungering and thirsting after righteousness; iniquity, though so hateful and hurtful, is regarded in the heart, but there is no regard unto God there. How can there be a worse distraction than for the heart to forsake fullness and goodness itself, and to embrace and fix upon mere emptiness and evil! In this distraction there is frenzy in the highest degree.

PARTICULAR 7. The heart is distracted when carnal self and interest in attending upon God is the great end designed. The end is that which directs an action; and the eye and heart of him who acts is upon the end which he pursues. If the end is wrong, the action cannot be right. Without a sincere aim, no religious duty can sincerely be performed. Now if we look no higher than our carnal selves in those services we pretend to do for God, our selfish design will be in our thoughts and will distract them. Acceptance with God, and the enjoyment of Him, will not be at all minded. The captives in Babylon were blamed in their fasting and mourning that God was not in their eye. His approbation and His glory were not regarded. Zechariah 7:5: "Did ye at all fast unto me, even to me?" They minded returning to Canaan more than returning to God and to their duty. If indeed we are truly selfish, God will not be angry with us; for there is an inseparable connection between God's honor and our truest interest. When we seek and eye Him most, we most truly eye and seek ourselves. God has the highest honor from us when we look for the highest happiness in Him, love Him for Himself, delight in Him, and bless and magnify Him to eternity. But when God Himself is not our end, but His service is made use of that we may better bring about our earthly and worldly designs and projects, our duties then are hypocrisy and distraction. Such were those whom the prophet so severely taxed. Jeremiah 12:2: "Thou art near in their mouth, and far from their reins." They spoke good words, but their hearts were far from that God to whom they spoke. It was outward prosperity and plenty that they sought; and this plenty and prosperity was most wickedly abused.

PARTICULAR 8. The heart is distracted when the worship performed is will worship of man's invention, not of God's institution. How can there but be distraction if we wander out of the way in which He has appointed us to serve Him? The Jews of old were very culpable in this respect. Isaiah 29:13: "Their fear toward me," said God, "is taught by the precept of men." When man aspired to be like God in wisdom, he deprived himself of the knowledge of God, and grew unacquainted with His will, so that he is utterly unfit to be his own instructor in religion. There is a necessity of a revelation from heaven so that God may be known; and the right way of serving Him may be understood. The vilest impurities, the greatest cruelties have been practiced under the name of devotion, when man has been contriving how God should be served. Nay, "will worship" is condemned by the apostle, though there is never so great a show of wisdom and humility, and neglecting of the body (Colossians 2:23). The will of God is to determine what worship pleases Him, not the will of man; and whatever mortifications and austerities some may fancy, God allows an honor and satisfaction to the flesh as long as the lusts of it are not fulfilled. Worship that is not of God's institution is mere distraction; it is labor to no purpose, unless it is to ill purpose. When God is represented by images, He is grossly misrepresented; the glory of Him who is an incorruptible Spirit is changed. When other mediators in heaven are made use of besides that great High Priest who has passed into heaven, Jesus the Son of God, worship becomes carnal and sinful, and the mind of the worshipper, instead of drawing near to God, is distracted and drawn away from Him.

CHAPTER 12

How to Attend upon God without Distraction

Second, I am to tell you what it is to attend upon the Lord without distraction.

1. To attend without distraction is to set God just before us, and ourselves just before God; it is when our eye is fixed upon His eye, and we behold Him looking most steadfastly upon us. He searches the hearts and weighs the spirits of the children of men. Nothing can escape His finding out, "for he knoweth the secrets of the heart" (Psalm 44:21). "Doth not he see my ways?" asked Job; not only the ways of the feet, but the ways and workings of his very soul were open to God's view. "We are all here present before God," said Cornelius in Acts 10:33. "I have set the LORD always before me," said David in Psalm 16:8. Undistracted attendance is when the Lord is still kept in our view, and when we keep and behave ourselves as under the inspection of the all-observing eye of His holiness.

2. To attend without distraction is to have right apprehensions of God whom we attend upon. God is a Spirit, and as such He must be apprehended when we worship Him, so that we may worship Him in spirit and in truth, and that our conceptions of Him may be spiritual and suitable to His nature. As He is without passions to which men are subject, so He is without

those bodily parts that men have. Indeed, metaphorically, eyes, hands, feet, and heart are in Scripture ascribed unto God; but these signify His knowledge, His working, His arriving and departing, His will and pleasure. We must take heed of entertaining gross ideas and images in our minds concerning God. Acts 17:29: "We ought not to think that the Godhead is like unto gold, or silver, or stone, graven by art and man's device." Such representations are very improper of Him, who not only fills the earth, but the heaven of heavens cannot contain Him. Our worship is distraction, and the heart is drawn away from God unto a mere vanity and idol, if God is conceived in the likeness of any creature. How severely were the Gentiles censured, and how dreadfully were they punished and left to their vile lusts and affections, to dishonor their own bodies, because they glorified not God as God, but changed His glory into the image of corruptible creatures. Romans 1:21–23: "Because that, when they knew God, they glorified him not as God, neither were thankful; but became vain in their imaginations, and their foolish heart was darkened. Professing themselves to be wise, they became fools, and changed the glory of the incorruptible God into an image made like to corruptible man, and to birds, and four-footed beasts, and creeping things."

In our attendance upon God, we must think of Him as an incomprehensible Spirit, of infinite wisdom, power, truth, holiness, mercy, and goodness; as ready in Christ to receive returning sinners, but full of displeasure against those who go on still in their trespasses. God must be believed to be One, yet in the unity there is a Trinity. This one God is Father, Son, and Holy Ghost. Gregory Nazianzen, an ancient Greek father, thus expressed his apprehensions of God when he came to worship Him: "I am not able to apprehend One, but I am presently struck with the brightness of Three. I am not able to distinguish

Three, but I am presently brought back to One again." Regulate your apprehensions of God by that revelation He has made of Himself in His own Word; and pry no farther than what is written so that you may undistractedly worship God Himself, and not the fruit of your imaginations instead of Him.

3. To attend without distraction implies the greatest intention of mind. As all the lines from the circumference of a circle meet together in one point of the center, so the thoughts of the mind should center upon God, and the duty that is done to Him. God should be so minded that all other things should be out of mind. Though the soul is united to the body, yet it should be in a sense separated, as risen with Christ and with Him ascended, and sitting in heavenly places. Ephesians 2:6: "And hath raised us up together, and made us sit together in heavenly places in Christ Jesus." How intent upon God and His praises are the spirits of just men made perfect! And the spirits of saints militant should imitate those who are triumphant. It is said of that famous mathematician Archimedes that when Syracuse was taken by Marcellus, he was so intent in making figures upon the ground that he did not notice the taking of the city, and was slain by a soldier who did not know who he was, for Marcellus had given a command to save him. If such a danger could not disturb the intention of Archimedes to save a city, the saving of a soul justly claims a greater intention in every duty we perform for God.

4. To attend without distraction implies the highest concern of the soul. Faith should be strong, and should constrain the mind to be serious; things invisible should be represented as so evident and substantial as if they were most visible and apparent. God should be addressed as if He appeared to us as He did to Abraham; as if He talked with us as He did to the children

of Israel from Mount Sinai. With humbleness of mind and self-abasement, considering our distance, guilt, and vileness, we should cry out, "Let not the Lord be angry. If we entreat the forgiveness of sin, and that our souls may live before Him!" Now we should stir up ourselves and take hold of God (Isaiah 64:7). Now His strength, His Son, and His covenant may be laid hold of; within a little while it may be too late, and impossible to do it. We should be concerned in all duties, and perform them with such a solicitous care as if we saw the dart of the last enemy ready to pierce us, and the grave open for us; as if we saw the Judge upon the great white throne, and all both small and great standing before God, and the books opened, that they might be "judged…according to their works" (Revelation 20:11–12). There should be a concern of spirit, as if we saw the world in a flame, hell naked before us, and we beheld the flashings of eternal fire, as if we saw heaven opened, and all the glory that is there. Weight, worth, and necessity command our concern. Now when we attend on God, we draw nigh to Him about those things that are of most absolute necessity, and of the greatest worth and weight imaginable.

5. To attend without distraction implies the fullest bent and inclination of heart; there must be a strong propensity of the will towards God, and this is expressed by longing and by panting. Psalm 42:1: "As the hart panteth after the water brooks, so panteth my soul after thee, O God." It is the Lord Himself who thus determines the will towards Himself. And this He does without compulsion; for He alters the nature and inclination of it so that the will, being made free by divine grace, uses its liberty aright, and chooses God as its end and the way of His testimonies. Such an end, such a way is most worthy to be chosen. The heart now desires the enjoyment of fellowship with God, as infinitely more valuable than all other

enjoyments. And this full bent of the heart mightily fixes it so that the stream of the affections is kept the better in one undivided channel. When the psalmist said that there was none on earth he desired besides God, it plainly showed that his desire after God swallowed up his desire after worldly things. And when he asks, "Whom have I in heaven but thee?" he signifies that he should not count heaven itself to be heaven without the enjoyment of God there.

6. To attend without distraction implies a sincere care to please the Lord in that attendance, His approval being principally minded. Man's good thoughts and words are more easily gained, but the Jew inwardly, his "praise is not of men, but of God" (Romans 2:29). And indeed all other commendations are insignificant unless the Lord commends (2 Corinthians 10:18). The undistracted attendant studies to approve himself to God. With what confidence does David speak before his all-discerning Judge, that he has walked in his integrity (Psalm 26:1)? Psalm 17:3: "Thou hast proved mine heart; thou hast visited me in the night; thou hast tried me, and shalt find nothing." He was not conscious of regarded sin, or of allowed guile and negligence in the Lord's service. Care to please that God whom we serve is a necessary ingredient in every service that is acceptable. This care commands the heart into the presence of God and keeps it there; and He loves to see hearts set on Him and seeking after Him.

7. To attend without distraction implies resisting all attempts to draw the heart away from God. Satan and mammon will be knocking at the door of the heart while it is attending upon the Lord, and the flesh that lusts against the Spirit will be apt to show its treachery and to open the door. Undistracted attendants use great vigilance, for they are full of jealousy

over themselves. They bid Satan to get behind them for they are worshipping the Lord their God, and it is wickedness and boldness in him to disturb them in the Lord's service; and when the affairs of the world would crowd in upon them, they reply that they have some greater and more important affairs to mind, and therefore those worldly matters must be regarded only at a convenient season. At all times it should be our care to keep unspotted from the world, to keep ourselves so that the wicked one does not touch us (1 John 5:18). But this care should be greatest when our approaches to God are nearest. For if the world and its god should bespatter and defile us, even while we are engaged in holy ordinances, how uncomely would this be! How inexcusable would we be! How displeased would the Lord be!

8. To attend without distraction implies refusing to be diverted from attending upon God without great necessity. Indeed, since the Lord will have mercy and not sacrifice, He will excuse our attendance when unavoidable necessity and the mercy He requires us to show divert us from it; but hearts that are truly gracious are troubled when they are thus diverted. When our Lord admonished His disciples to pray that their flight might not be in the winter, nor on the Sabbath day (Matthew 24:20), He plainly intimated that to be disturbed on the Sabbath, and to be hindered from engaging in ordinances, ought to be looked upon as a very great affliction. Carnal minds are glad of occasions that seem to justify their omission of holy duties; but sanctified and renewed hearts are otherwise minded. They are sensible that worship and duty are owed to the Lord, and that He does not benefit, but they, by their giving it. The farm, the merchandise, and things of that nature cannot hinder their coming to the marriage supper. They are deaf to the persuasions of carnal relations and friends who would

draw them off from exercises of religion. They know that time was given them, not that they should chiefly mind temporal things, but those things that are invisible and eternal. To be far from God is the way to perish; it is good, it is pleasant, and it is safe to be near Him (Psalm 73:27–28). To be diverted from attending on the Lord is to be diverted from the most blessed thing on earth. Psalm 65:4: "Blessed is the man whom thou choosest, and causest to approach unto thee, that he may dwell in thy courts: we shall be satisfied with the goodness of thy house, even of thy holy temple."

9. To attend without distraction implies abiding with God, and perseverance in His service. The undistracted attendant is steadfast in the Lord's covenant. His bonds and cords are bonds and cords of love; and why should any say, "Let us break these bonds asunder and cast away these cords from us"? The words in Jeremiah 50:5 were good words, and they who spoke them were as good as their word: "They shall ask the way to Zion with their faces thitherward, saying, Come, and let us join ourselves to the LORD in a perpetual covenant that shall not be forgotten." This perpetual covenant should be kept in everlasting remembrance; and there is good reason for it. Psalm 25:10: "All the paths of the LORD are mercy and truth unto such as keep his covenant and his testimonies." He who attends without distraction does not cease to be an attendant, but perseveres in his Lord's service. He takes care to have his loins girded for spiritual labor and his light burning, for he is awaiting and expecting his Lord's coming. An ancient father wished that when Christ came He might find him either praying or preaching. Every Christian should have a wish of this nature, that he may be found either praying, hearing, or practicing what he hears. "Blessed is that servant, whom his lord when he cometh shall find so doing" (Luke 12:43).

CHAPTER 13

The Evils of Distractions and Benefits of Avoiding Them

Third, I am to assign the reasons why, with such care, we should take heed of distraction in the Lord's service. These reasons shall be of two sorts: The first sort shall be drawn from the evil of distraction. The second sort shall be drawn from the benefit of attending without distraction.

The first sort of reasons shall be drawn from the evil of distraction, and the evil of this I shall make manifest and apparent:

REASON 1. In distraction there is great irreverence and contempt of God. "Wherefore doth the wicked contemn God?" asks the psalmist in Psalm 10:13. There is no reason why he should do it; nay, there is all the reason in the world to the contrary, that he should adore and serve Him. The wicked contemn God by running away from Him, and by a total neglect of His service; but His attendants contemn Him when they make their addresses to Him if, instead of offering spiritual sacrifices, they offer affronts to God, and there is a special offensiveness in so doing. Therefore He protests that such services were a trouble to Him, that He was weary of bearing them, and that His soul hated them (Isaiah 1:14). If a man should address an earthly potentate, and instead of speaking to the king should occasionally talk to some inferior person who stood by; if instead of hearing the king he should turn his eye and his ear away from him, and not mind a word he should say—the royal majesty would look upon this as an insufferable affront. But thus, in distracted duties, the King of glory is treated; the mind is upon the creature, and this and that and the other worldly affair, when the tongue is speaking to the Creator. What He speaks, many times the ear does not hear, and the heart is farther off from heeding. Thus, what would not be done to a governor is done to the highest, best, and greatest King, of whose dreadful name all the earth should stand in awe.

REASON 2. In distraction we take God's name in vain; the third commandment is broken, the transgressors whereof the Lord says He will not hold guiltless (Exodus 20:7). This may be called the first commandment with a threat, as the fifth is said to be the first commandment with promise; for though in the second commandment mention is made of the mercy of God and of His jealousy, yet jealousy is provoked by them who hate God while the other is promised to them who love Him and keep His commandments. Only the third commandment specifies a threat for a particular action. To what purpose is a duty performed where distraction is allowed? The name of God is not hallowed but profaned when it sounds from the lips, and the heart thinks not of nor sanctifies Him whose name is spoken. When distraction prevails, all ordinances are engaged in vain; nay, not only do we miss the benefit that is promised unto serious engagers, but guilt is contracted; and by such distracted duties the distance becomes greater between God and the performers. Bernard complained, "I sing and pray one thing, and think another." And afterwards, "I commit faults, woe is me! even in those duties by which my faults should be amended." It was well that he said, "Woe is me!" because of these distractions;

else God would have said, "Woe to thee" because of them. And indeed, where they are not minded nor bewailed, the case is woeful. God takes it amiss, and is very much displeased, that such hypocrites take His name into their mouths.

REASON 3. In distraction there is a slighting of Jesus, the Advocate and Mediator. Our Lord's heart and soul were in the work of our redemption. He was forward to undertake it. Hebrews 10:7: "Lo, I come...to do thy will, O God." And He was just as willing to finish it; therefore in His greatest agonies He said, "Not my will, but thine be done." His holy will, notwithstanding the reluctance of innocent nature, perfectly submitted to His Father's pleasure. John 18:11: "The cup which my Father giveth me to drink, shall I not drink it?" How undistracted and fervent was our Lord in praying for His church, whom His Father had given Him out of the world! And now that He is in heaven, His heart, thoughts, and cares are upon and for His militant members below. His intercession for them is incessant. His life now in heaven is a life of continual interceding; and the end of His intercession is that the blessings He has purchased by His sufferings may be bestowed upon believers for whom He suffered.

Now what a slight is put upon this great High Priest who has passed into the heavens, where he is so serious to intercede, if we are not serious in petitioning; if we hardly think of what we are doing when we are asking for those blessings which cost Him not only strong cries and tears, but His blood and life to purchase! They were not small things that the blood of God was a price to purchase; they are not small things that a glorified Redeemer is continually praying to the Father to bestow. If these things are scarcely thought of when we ask for them, they are most sinfully undervalued. Christ Himself, His fullness, His satisfaction, and His intercession are all despised altogether.

REASON 4. In distraction there is a grieving and vexing of the Holy Spirit of God by not valuing His preferred assistance. When Christ ascended into heaven and was glorified there, He sent the Spirit to abide with His church forever. And one great work of the Spirit is to aid and assist us in our supplications. He urges us to attend upon God, and is most ready to help us in that attendance. He is ready to fix our minds, to incline our hearts aright, to enlarge our desire, and to "make intercession for us with groanings which cannot be uttered" (Romans 8:26). He offers us His mighty grace, which will enable us to pray prevailingly, to hear profitably, and fruitfully to improve the ordinances of God. But distracted attendants are a grief and vexation to this good Spirit; they would rather be without His help and grace than have it. They choose rather to lose all their duties by a wretched heartlessness and formality than to be assisted to take pains in these duties that they may fare the better for them forever.

REASON 5. In distraction there is an undervaluing of all the promised mercies and blessings that God is ready to bestow on them who seriously attend upon Him. The promises of the gospel are made by Him whose faithfulness never fails; and the Surety of the New Testament stands engaged that they shall be accomplished, if they are applied by a true and lively faith. These promises are of things that without which will make us miserable beyond conception! Peace with God through Christ; and that peace within that passes all understanding; grace sufficient to succor, support, strengthen, and establish; the good things of this life, with a blessing from heaven upon them, and endless blessedness in the world to come—these are the things that are promised; and who besides God can make promises so exceedingly precious and so great? Now in our attendance upon Him, He would have us expect what He has promised, for He keeps truth forever, and what He has promised He is able to perform (Romans 4:21). Distracted attendants upon the Lord look upon these promises with a strange eye; they either do not believe the truth of them or are not persuaded of the worth of them, and are very careless in pleading them. And having no serious thoughts and desires after the promised blessings, the threatened curses fall upon them.

REASON 6. In distraction there is great carelessness of ourselves and our main concerns, those of our immortal souls. In attendance upon God, our souls are principally concerned. Now these souls themselves are of more worth than the world, and so are the blessings we request for them. And to be heartless and trifling here, what apology can be made for it? What has come to the soul of man that it should be so mindless of itself, that it should have so few thoughts about itself! Distracted duties argue an indifference toward what becomes of the precious soul to eternity; and an indifference must cause a miscarriage and ruin, since striving to enter in at the strait gate is necessary, and heaven will be missed if there is not a holy violence to take it. In distracted services men cheat themselves; they only seem to run, and so they will really miss the prize. And in this distraction there is great hypocrisy, which is most hateful to God, and which our Lord has denounced so many woes against. Hypocrites' duties are a most provoking mockery; and though hell will have all the wicked at last turned into it, yet in a special manner it is called the portion of hypocrites as well as unbelievers (Matthew 24:51 compared with Luke 12:46).

REASON 7. Distraction exposes us to Satan. Distracted attendants are servants of the Lord only in show, but Satan is really served and gratified by their duties. They expose themselves to this enemy as both an accuser and a tempter. When their hearts are absent from the Lord's work in which they engage, Satan's mouth is open against them. He boldly charged Job with being a mercenary servant, and yet there was no ground for it. Job 1:9: "Doth Job fear God for nought?" But "put forth thine hand now, and touch all that he hath, and he will curse thee to thy face" (verse 11). And if he charged so good and upright a man without ground, surely he will be forward to accuse when there is abundant ground for the accusation. "See," Satan will say, "how such and such serve the Lord with duties that are things of nought, and good for nothing. See how they mock the God of heaven to His very face." And upon such distracted service, as he is forward to be an accuser, so he has great advantage as a tempter. Such poorly performed duties bring in no strength from above to withstand him. Nay, the Lord is provoked to withdraw further; and those whom God leaves to themselves, how easily Satan leads them captive at his pleasure! All strays are seized by the god of this world; how close then should we cleave to the God of heaven!

REASON 8. Distraction is a great obstruction to the efficacy and success of ordinances. If we pray as if we prayed not, shall we succeed? If we hear as if we heard not, shall we profit? Will doing the work of the Lord deceitfully be encouraged by the vouchsafing of grace or rewarded with glory? Carefulness is one effect and fruit of godly sorrow. 2 Corinthians 7:11: "For behold this selfsame thing, that ye sorrowed after a godly sort, what carefulness it wrought in you." And as I said before, this carefulness is an ingredient in every acceptable duty. The distracted attendant has little care that God may be pleased; he does not care that ordinances, in a spiritual sense, are beneficial to him. God's anger therefore remains and abides upon him; nay, He grows more angry because of his negligence.

Ordinances leave him as they found him, not at all safer or better. Nay, the Word, not being a savor of life to life, proves to be a savor of death to death (2 Corinthians 2:16). 'Tis sad to have the means of salvation ineffectual to salvation; but 'tis worse, by these very means of salvation being distractedly used, to have destruction promoted.

And thus have I made apparent those evils that are the result of distraction. The second sort of reasons shall be drawn from the benefits of attending upon the Lord without distraction. The benefit of such kind of attendance I shall make manifest.

REASON 1. Attenders without distraction have hearts that are right with God. He is, in Christ, well pleased with them, and with their serious services. That which the Lord chiefly minds and calls for, it is their care to give to Him, and that is their very heart. The Lord rejoiceth in the habitable parts of the earth, and His delights are with the sons of men (Proverbs 8:31), the sons of men who seek Him, and whose hearts are perfect with Him. As the wicked man himself is hateful, so the "sacrifice of the wicked is an abomination to the LORD," because he never offers his heart. God is not in his thoughts even when he is offering sacrifice to Him, but "the prayer of the upright is his delight" (Proverbs 15:8). The Heart-searcher sees how his heart and his words agree together. The Lord is very much pleased to behold the thoughts called off from other things, because He is preferred before them all; to behold the mind fixed upon Himself, and the soul with great vigor desiring His grace, His strength, and His salvation, as that which is most worthy to be longed for. That is the language of heaven to such a one. Song of Solomon 2:14: "Let me see thy countenance, let me hear thy voice; for sweet is thy voice, and thy countenance is comely."

REASON 2. Attenders without distraction draw very near to God. And if it is so good to draw near to Him, it follows then that the nearer the better. There are some whom the Lord beholds afar off, those whose proud and hard hearts were never truly humbled for sin. Their iniquity is a wall of partition between God and them. When the spouse of Christ herself was given to sleep, though her heart waked and was loathe and lazy in too great a degree in seeking her Lord, she complained thus: "My beloved had withdrawn himself, and was gone…I sought him, but could not find him; I called him, but he gave me no answer" (Song of Solomon 5:6). But undistracted attendance shows great diligence, vehemence of desire, and truth in the inward parts. And God is nigh to them who call upon Him in truth. He is nigh to them not in some things only, but in all that they call upon Him for (Deuteronomy 4:7). God is nigh as one reconciled, as one nearly related, as a most compassionate and ready helper, as a sure shield and buckler, as a full and all-sufficient fountain, from whom whatever is needed may be derived.

REASON 3. Attenders without distraction know still more of God; they come to be more intimately acquainted with Him, and that acquaintance is, of all others, the most high and beneficial. Job 22:21: "Acquaint now thyself with him, and be at peace: thereby good shall come unto thee." To understand the secrets of nature; to understand human affairs and how they may be most prudently ordered; to understand the ordinances of heaven, the motions and influences of the sun, moon, and stars, are pieces of knowledge very desirable—but to know the Lord Himself is a wisdom far beyond all other. The undistracted attendant follows on to know the Lord, and gives himself more entirely to His service; and God will manifest Himself to such a one in a more peculiar way. Psalm 25:14:

"The secret of the LORD is with them that fear him; and he will show them his covenant." And their knowledge shall not be only theoretical, but, to their great satisfaction, it shall be experiential. While others only hear of God by the hearing of the ear, they shall taste and see that He is gracious. Psalm 34:8–10: "O taste and see that the LORD is good: blessed is the man that trusteth in him. O fear the LORD, ye his saints: for there is no want to them that fear him. The young lions do lack, and suffer hunger: but they that seek the LORD shall not want any good thing."

REASON 4. Attenders without distraction have most of the grace of God, and the greatest strength from Him. The Lord gives grace that is greater than the greatest earthly things, or He "giveth more grace" (James 4:6). Still more and more He is ready to communicate, and most of all to them who are most humble and who draw nearest to Him. Such as are bent to seek the Lord, His strength, and His face evermore shall not seek Him, His face, or strength in vain. Holy David, who was a sincere seeker, declared the good success he had in Psalm 138:3: "In the day when I cried thou answeredst me, and strengthenedst me with strength in my soul." And as the strength of God rested on him, so the face of God shone upon him to his great consolation. Psalm 21:5–6: "His glory is great in thy salvation.... For thou hast made him most blessed forever: thou hast made him exceeding glad with thy countenance." The undistracted attendant thrives; he grows rich in faith, rich in assurance, and rich in experience. He increases with the increases of God; he grows up into Him in all things who is his Head, and approaches still nearer to the measure of the stature of the fullness of Christ. And where there is the most grace, usually there is the most peace and joy, perfecting holiness in the fear of God; and the comforts of the Holy Ghost commonly keep pace, and go hand in hand together.

REASON 5. Attenders without distraction are most victorious over their spiritual enemies. Being strong in the Lord, and in the power of His might, the power of the enemies of their salvation can prevail but little. The nearer any approach unto God, the farther they come out from the world; and they are the more fortified against it, both on the right hand and on the left, the less they notice the world's honor or dishonor, evil report or good report from it. They are not afraid of the world's terror, and whatever the world offers to them, they see enough in God to make the highest earthly enjoyments despised in comparison. Thus the innumerable multitude of stars, though never so glittering before, all disappear at the sun's rising. Undistracted attenders fix their eye on God, and the more the invisible God is seen, the more all visible things will vanish into nothing. The psalmist had cast his eye upon the prosperity of the wicked, and began to admire it; then he came into the sanctuary of God, and, looking upon God, he wondered at his own folly in admiring so poor a thing as worldly happiness. And the temptation that was so strong was overcome. Safety from the most dangerous enemies is of the Lord; they whose thoughts are upon His name find it to be a strong tower. Satan and mammon are less able to beguile them, and the lustings of the flesh become weaker and weaker against the Spirit. And as they find sin more and more destroyed, so they may behold the last enemy, death, without a sting, and the grave as having lost its victory.

REASON 6. Attenders without distraction have the most approbation from their own consciences. Conscience is a monitor unto duty, and a diligent observer of how it is performed.

It will condemn laziness; it will commend labor of love; it will upbraid the evil and slothful with their vain oblations. But to the undistracted attendant it will say, "Well done, good and faithful servant!" And how much joy and peace are there in the testimony of a good conscience! In 2 Corinthians 1:12 we find a condemning and an approving conscience compared; the condemning conscience is the forerunner of God's condemning, and the approbation of the conscience is the forerunner of God's absolution. First John 3:20–21: "If our heart condemn us, God is greater than our heart, and knoweth all things. Beloved, if our heart condemn us not, then have we confidence toward God." Duties come off with great comfort when we have been intent and affected, when God has been attentive to us, when we behold His face shining and find His hand open; and conscience bears us witness that we have been seriously (and the Lord has been graciously) minding what we have been doing.

REASON 7. Attenders without distraction are the most beneficial to others. They have the most public spirits, and all fare the better for that interest they have in heaven, which they daily improve for all. How much is the church of God beholden to them who will not hold their peace day or night, who will give the Lord no rest until He makes Jerusalem a praise on the earth (Isaiah 62:6–7)! When the wickedness of Israel had made a great breach for the wrath of God to break in upon them to consume them, Moses attended upon God and interceded with such intention, concern, and fervency that the wrath of God was appeased and the ruin prevented, though it was at the door. Psalm 106:23: "Therefore he said that he would destroy them, had not Moses his chosen stood before him in the breach, to turn away his wrath, lest he should destroy them." Whole nations reap the benefit of such undistracted and prevailing intercessions. The apostle tells us that Elijah was a man of like passions with others, yet he was so intent and fervent in prayer that he opened heaven and fetched rain. He says that the earth brought forth her fruit, and an end was put to a terrible famine, which had lasted for several years. James 5:16: "The effectual fervent prayer of a righteous man availeth much," for he prevails for others as well as for himself. Lot was a righteous man, and vexed his righteous soul because of the Sodomites' unlawful deeds (2 Peter 2:8); yet his deliverance from Sodom's flames was ascribed unto Abraham's intercession. Genesis 19:29: "And it came to pass, when God destroyed the cities of the plain, that God remembered Abraham, and sent Lot out of the midst of the overthrow, when he overthrew the cities wherein Lot dwelt." Saints should pray harder one for another, and pray for them who are outside the faith, with more earnestness so that greater multitudes may be called out of the world and brought into the church, and secured from the perdition of ungodly men. Undistracted attendants upon God are pillars to bear up what otherwise would fall into ruin. The church, the nation in which they live, even the whole world is beholden to them, as well as particular persons for whom they are concerned, and whom they bear upon their hearts before the Lord.

PART FOUR

Cases of Conscience and Applications of Attending upon God without Distractions

CHAPTER 14

Cases of Conscience about Distractions

I am to answer some cases of conscience about these distractions in attending upon God, so that difficulties which are apt to perplex the mind in this matter may be removed.

CASE 1. Is it possible that the thoughts cannot be off from God in the least when we attend upon Him, without there necessarily being a culpable and sinful distraction?

ANSWER. In all our holy duties, from beginning to end, there should be a constant overawing sense of God upon our spirits. Slavish fear alienates the heart from God, but filial reverence keeps the heart close to Him. That part of the duty is lost in which the sense of God is banished.

Something else besides God may be thought of in duties, and yet this is not distraction. To think of our sins when we confess them is our duty, and to recollect the circumstances by which they have been heightened and rendered more exceeding sinful. Isaiah 59:12: "For our transgressions are multiplied before thee, and our sins testify against us: for our transgressions are with us; and as for our iniquities, we know them." We ought to think of our wants, and the necessity of having them supplied; and the all-sufficient Jehovah is sufficient to supply all needs whatsoever, be they never so great and many, and the persons who apply to Him never so vast a multitude. The blessings we desire ought also to be thought of. Others also whom we pray for may be in our minds when we are before God, with their distresses, under which we would fain be helpful to them by our supplications on their behalf. It was no distraction in the apostle, but a matter of thanksgiving to the Lord, that when he was at the throne of grace, Timothy was in his thoughts and remembrance. 2 Timothy 1:3: "I thank God, whom I serve from my forefathers with pure conscience, that without ceasing I have remembrance of thee in my prayers night and day."

Our thoughts must not run out so much upon the matter of our duties, but that there must be a quick and continual return to God, the object whom we worship. We must not so much be thinking what we are praying for, but we must ever be minding Him whom we are praying to. The psalmist says in Psalm 142:2, "I poured out my complaint before Him; I shewed before him my trouble." He thought of his trouble, but he also had a sense that he was before God, who he knew could be a present help to him.

CASE 2. Is it a distraction and withdrawing from God to think at all of our worldly business and affairs?

ANSWER. In ordering our earthly concerns, and in all our ways, God is to be acknowledged. His direction makes us act prudently, and His blessing makes our labor prosperous. "The blessing of the LORD, it maketh rich, and he addeth no sorrow with it" (Proverbs 10:22). His blessing removes the curse which sin had brought, and very much cures the vexatious vanity of the creature. The Word of God is to be eyed as the rule by which we ought to walk in our secular affairs; we should inquire after His will, and aim at His glory in everything we do.

When secular actions are under the conduct and management of religion, there is not only a blessing upon them, but also a great beauty in them.

Diligence and prudence in our worldly affairs are duties, and these cannot be without thoughts about them. Honest projects and wise contrivances are not at all to be discommended; what is said of the husbandman's skill is applicable to discretion in any other calling. Isaiah 28:26, 29: "God doth instruct him to discretion, and doth teach him." A prudent thoughtfulness in these matters "cometh from the Lord of hosts, which is wonderful in counsel, and excellent in working." To be without heed and care in the works of our calling is sinful and scandalous, and to walk disorderly. Our Lord plainly signifies that there must be care and fidelity in worldly things. Luke 16:11: "If therefore ye have not been faithful in the unrighteous mammon, who will commit to your trust the true riches?" The good man must think of his secular affairs, else he could not guide them with discretion.

In a special manner we are to take heed, when engaged in worldly business, of being too long without thinking of God and lifting up our hearts to Him. Worldly men, when they are in the sanctuary and seem to be worshipping the God of heaven, their thoughts are upon the world because their affections run that way. Thus the saints should do when at the exchange, in their shops, or at the market: their hearts even then should frequently be with God. This would not be hypocrisy but sincerity in them, and worldly business would succeed the better for it. Psalm 143:8 is a proper prayer at every turn in our secular matters: "Cause me to know the way wherein I should walk; for I lift up my soul unto thee." And our ordinary employments, though never so advantageous and delightful, should not be so consuming, but that with the greatest readiness and joy we should cease from them when called to give our attendance upon God.

CASE 3. Can the best of men while in this world be totally free from distraction in holy duties?

ANSWER. The natural vanity of the imagination is not perfectly cured in any saint alive, and this vanity in some degree will discover itself; the most serious and solid mind has something of levity and frothiness in it, and this froth will be working up, notwithstanding all endeavors to suppress it. Evil is present with the best when they would do their very best. The apostle acknowledged that there was a law of sin in him. Indwelling sin remains even where grace reigns, and is but too active in the saints when they desire to be most active in the Lord's service. Therefore we read that the most spiritual sacrifices are acceptable through Jesus Christ (1 Peter 2:5). Though the house is spiritual, the priesthood holy, and the sacrifice spiritual, yet all this by itself cannot procure acceptance. There are some sinful imperfections, some ebullitions of vanity, as well as actings of grace, which, to cover, there is great need of the mediation and righteousness of the Lord Jesus.

Saints are not so vigilant, and do not take such pains with their hearts, as they ought and might do, and before they are aware of it they are distracted in their thoughts. The sluggard's field was all grown over with thorns, and nettles had covered the face thereof (Proverbs 24:31). The heart of man by nature brings forth nothing but weeds; and though the heart is renewed, yet these weeds will presently spring up in it if the heart is not kept with constant care.

Though believers are still haunted and pestered with some vain thoughts, yet it is possible for them to be freed more and more from them. The more they are renewed in the spirit of their mind, they will be able to serve the Lord with greater intention of mind and seriousness of spirit. The more your reason gets power over your fancy, the more grace gets power over your reason, and the more you call in help from heaven, the more fixed your hearts will be upon God and His work. Taking pains with the heart in duty is hard labor, but the Lord is ready to make it succeed.

CASE 4. May not a true believer sometimes perform duties so distractedly as to reap no benefit at all by them?

ANSWER. The more there is of distraction in duties, the less spiritual advantage is likely to be reaped by them; the more frequently the heart starts away from God when it is engaged in His worship, the more obstruction there is unto the communication of grace. The nearer we draw to God, the nearer He draws to us; if we at any time withdraw, it is no wonder if He withdraws likewise. And the less a saint is troubled at his own distractions, his heart is certainly in the worse frame, and God is the more displeased.

Some duties may be so distractedly performed as to be totally lost. It is true that the union between Christ and believers is inseparable, and nothing shall separate them from the love of God in Him; for He makes incessant intercession for all His members. It is also certain that the Spirit abides in all true believers and will never quite leave them who are His temples and habitation. And since the Spirit ever dwells in them, they shall ever continue in a state of grace, and sin shall never recover its dominion over them. Yet sometimes they may fall into particular acts of sin, and some particular duties may be performed in such a careless and distracted manner as to become sin. We read in Psalm 80:4: "O LORD God of hosts, how long wilt thou be angry with the prayer of thy people?" Prayers of saints may be unacceptable. Sometimes unbelief, despondence, discontent, and impatience quite spoil prayer. How could the Lord be pleased with Jonah's petition? Jonah 4:2–3: "And he prayed unto the LORD, and said, I pray thee, O LORD, was not this my saying, when I was yet in my country? Therefore I fled before unto Tarshish: for I knew that thou art a gracious God, and merciful, slow to anger, and of great kindness, and repentest thee of the evil. Therefore now, O LORD, take, I beseech thee, my life from me; for it is better for me to die than to live." Sometimes distraction, deadness, and a carnal, worldly frame of spirit may hinder a duty from doing any good to the one who performs it, though he is good in the main. The perfection of sincerity may be so wanting in some services that they may prove to be of no avail. Revelation 3:2: "Be watchful, and strengthen the things which remain, that are ready to die: for I have not found thy works perfect before God."

I add further that duties may be so performed by believers themselves that the bad manner of doing them shall cost them very dearly. A true saint may do his duty in a way so displeasing to God that his duty shall be his death. Thus the Corinthians came together to the Lord's Table, not for the better, but for the worse. There was not that care to keep their hearts fixed upon God and fit for communion with Him; the Holy Supper was profaned by a prevailing sensuality, and divine displeasure broke out against them. 1 Corinthians 11:30: "For this cause many are weak and sickly among you, and many sleep." They were thus chastened of the Lord, and some with stripes that proved deadly, that they might not be condemned with the world (verse 32). With what intention, vigilance, and godly fear should the Lord's people engage in His work and worship! He will be sanctified by them who draw near to Him, or He will be sanctified upon them. He will manifest to their cost what a holy and jealous God He is. Therefore the apostle said, "Do we provoke the Lord to jealousy? are we stronger than he?" (1 Corinthians 10:22).

CASE 5. What distractions are mercifully overlooked and do not hinder the success of our duties or the benefit of them?

ANSWER. The Lord in much compassion overlooks those distractions in His service that are grievous to us and that we heartily lament. He passes by the greatest sins for the great Propitiation's sake, if there is contrition in him who has been guilty of them. Psalm 51:17: "The sacrifices of God are a broken spirit: a broken and contrite heart, O God, thou wilt not despise." And if the heart is broken because religious duties are so broken and interrupted by vain imaginations, He will not withdraw His presence because of these weaknesses that are bewailed, but according to His promise He will be nigh to them that are of a broken heart, and will save such as are of a contrite spirit (Psalm 34:18).

Distractions shall be passed by that are prayed against before they come, and are resisted when they are come. He who would worship God with great intention of soul, it is a sign that his heart is good and honest; and that very will is wrought in him by the Lord's own grace, and is pleasing in the Lord's eyes. It is even further pleasing to Him when He beholds a soul checking these distractions as often as they occur, and manifesting a constant dislike of them. The psalmist tells us that he hated vain thoughts, but He loved both the Word and the work of God (Psalm 119:113). His hatred of vain thoughts was well taken; the intruding of them, though they were hated, was overlooked in mercy. And this hatred of them, and perpetual conflicting with them, is a good way to be rid of them. Certainly those distractions shall not be imputed to us which, by checking them and crying to heaven for help, we in some measure prevail against.

Distractions shall be overlooked, the causes of which we endeavor to remove—when we are on our guard against the cares of this life, deceitful riches, and those lusts and pleasures that would command our thoughts and entice our hearts away from God, and cause them to be absent when our bodies are before Him. It is mere self-deceit to pretend that we are desirous to be freed from the effect if we like the cause; we cannot say that we dislike distraction if we are pleased well enough with those things whereby distraction is caused. The psalmist, who sighed and said, "O let me not wander from thy commandments" (Psalm 119:10), certainly was watchful against and groaned to be delivered from everything that might make him wander. Therefore he wished that his heart might not be inclined to covetousness, and that his eyes might be turned away from beholding vanity (verses 36–37). He knew very well that coveting this world's wealth would eat out his desires after God, and that eyeing and affecting vanity would deaden and distract his heart in the Lord's service.

Distractions, though very horrid, shall not hinder the success of duties that the heart trembles at, and utterly detests and abhors the distraction. Satan sometimes apparently shows himself to be a devil indeed: he roars like a lion and speaks like the old dragon. Hideous, blasphemous injections and thoughts are with hellish violence cast into the mind of a believer who is attending upon God; the heart seems to be overspread with the blackness of darkness, and with the wickedness of hell itself. But when these satanic injections are disowned, and the believer cries out, "Lord, I am oppressed; undertake for me"; when his eye is unto Jesus for succor, who is so ready to help those who by force are ready to be run down by the devil (Acts 10:38), Satan shall not prevail against the believer, but the believer shall prevail with God for that grace of which the evil one is so busy to hinder him from partaking.

Distractions shall in pity be covered if they are occasioned by the prevailing indisposition of the head or other corporal maladies, if they are the effect of excessive pain or of melancholy, which causes great confusion. In such cases the Lord's compassion is drawn forth, rather than His displeasure provoked. We read in Psalm 103:13–14: "Like as a father pitieth his children, so the LORD pitieth them that fear him, for he knoweth our frame." They are subject to much bodily indisposition as well as to spiritual infirmities. Now what earthly father is angry with a child because he does not do those acts of obedience in sickness that he could and would readily do were his health continued? The Lord is infinitely beyond the tenderest earthly parent in pitying and sparing His children. He observes the spirit's willingness when the flesh is weak and indisposed.

Distractions by sudden accidents also shall not hinder the acceptance of duties. God will have mercy and not sacrifice (Matthew 9:13). It will not displease Him, neither shall duty be lost, if we leave off prayer to help one near us who has fallen into a swoon, and who may expire without speedy aid. In such cases His own providence calls us off from a duty of religion to an act of mercy.

Distractions shall be passed by that drive us to Christ for acceptance, and to the Spirit for greater assistance. Looking upon the defects in our services should make us look unto our Lord, in whom we are complete (Colossians 2:10), and rest with a more entire dependence upon His righteousness. Hereby Christ is honored, the Father pleased, and a multitude of faults will be covered. But help against them must be desired from the Holy Ghost. A gracious heart still desires renewed strength and aid from the Spirit to serve the Lord more acceptably; but a lazy reliance upon Christ, with an allowance of defects and distractions in the duties we perform, must be a very great provocation.

CASE 6. What course are melancholy persons to take in their attendance on God, when distractions arise from the prevalence of that distemper?

ANSWER. They should take heed of prolixity and length in holy duties. It is not length, but life in these duties that God looks at. It is a thought that may lodge in the breast of an heathen, but is unworthy of a Christian's heart, that he shall be heard for his "much speaking" (Matthew 6:7). Christians should not think much of the time they spend with God; yet overdoing in this regard is doing less than if less were done. When melancholy hinders duties from being extended, as formerly with vigor and fervency they were, they who more briefly now perform them should be the more frequent in short and holy petitions. And they must be sure to avoid taking more pains to fix their thoughts than their heads will bear; for when their heads are out of order, the more they labor to be intent, the further they are off from it; the disorder increases, and so does their discouragement. The Lord in such cases allows them to spare their pains, which are not only fruitless and hurtful; instead He calls on them to pity themselves, and not to attempt what a distempered brain is unfit for.

Melancholy ones must look to Jesus in the due use of means for the cure of head distempers. How many corporal maladies did our Lord heal in a miraculous manner when He was here on earth! And He has not put off His compassions toward the bodies of men now that He is in heaven. Though the skill of the lutist is never so great, he can never make good music if the lute itself is out of tune. Satan gains great advantage by prevailing melancholy to hinder devotion, by the disorder of the head, though the heart is never so honest and well-inclined. Our Lord very well knows this, and, being a merciful and faithful High Priest, He is ready to succor in this case also. All power is given to Him in earth as well as heaven, all judgment committed to Him (John 5:22), so that all distempers and diseases come and go at His command. And though miraculous cures are not now to be expected, yet something like them sometimes has been wrought in answer unto prayer and faith. And where there has been a steadfast looking to Jesus, a mighty blessing has attended the means that have been used for bringing blood, spirits, and brain into better order.

There are two great duties for which those who are under the power of melancholy are not so fit: the one is meditation, the other self-examination. A distempered and disordered head will make but sorry work of solemn meditation; the head will ache, the mind will be lost in a cloud and mist of confusion, and the evil one will be ready to strike and make the melancholy man turn into a self-accuser and, consequently, a self-tormentor. Such a one therefore should be wary of attempting the duty of set meditation; rather meditation and reading should be joined together. A short consideration of what is read there should be what the head can bear, a desire that the heart may be affected, and by the grace of God a resolution to act and walk accordingly. His petition should be, "Make me to go in the path of thy commandments.... Incline my heart unto thy testimonies" (Psalm 119:35–36).

As for self-examination, melancholy ones, being now not so well themselves, should not be forward nor peremptory in passing censures and judgment upon themselves; they should be aware that Satan is now busy about them, and, being a lying spirit, his suggestions that they are hypocrites and have no grace, that they are cast away and utterly forsaken by the God of all grace, should in no wise be credited. Satan's suggestions may be known by the design of them, which is not to quicken souls to duty, as the motions of the Holy Spirit are, but to drive them away from God, and to make them say, as he did in another case, since the case seemed desperate and all hope of salvation gone, "What should I wait for the Lord any longer?" (2 Kings 6:33).

Melancholy ones, in the midst of their distractions, should grieve that neither head nor heart is so disposed to serve the Lord as they desire. That is proper language to be used which came out of the mouth of holy Job in Job 10:15, "I am full of confusion; therefore see thou mine affliction." And since they cannot actively glorify God by the exercise of strong faith, vehement love, and joy and delight in God, they should glorify Him by a humble and patient submission to His will.

When a melancholy soul is quite emptied of all self-confidence, and self-conceit is in a manner annihilated; when under a great sense of its own guilt and vileness it looks unto Jesus, and desires by His blood and Spirit to be justified, washed, and made clean; when it is ready to acknowledge that if ever it is saved and brought to heaven, grace will be free and superabundant, because one of the lowest places in hell has been deserved—how far is flesh from glorying! And hereby glory is given to the Lord. When melancholy ones are ready in their greatest distractions and blackest darkness to justify the Lord as being righteous in all His ways and holy in all His works, and to condemn themselves because formerly, when their heads were in better order, their hearts were no better disposed and inclined to the Lord's service, they please and glorify Him more than they are aware of. The more there is of self-distrust, self-dislike, self-condemnation, humility, and patient bearing of divine indignation, because of sin that has been committed, the more honor by all this really redounds to God.

Let melancholy ones take heed of being quite staved off from duties and ordinances, though their performances are but poor and sorry. The Lord can discern sense in the soul when perhaps there is hardly sense in the words. He takes notice of the gracious bent and good inclination of the heart towards Himself when the thoughts unwillingly wander. Hezekiah had a most remarkable answer, and prayed to good purpose, when his petitions were broken and were rather chattering than supplications. Isaiah 38:14: "Like a crane or a swallow, so did I chatter: I did mourn as a dove: mine eyes fail with looking upward: O LORD, I am oppressed; undertake for me."

CASE 7. What are those distractions that make our attendance upon God altogether unacceptable to Him, and of no avail to ourselves?

ANSWER. Distractions make our duties of no effect if there is no concern that God observes them, as long as man can take no notice of them. How can it be expected that the Lord should have any gracious regard for them who have no regard for Him, or for His all-observing eye? They who mind the praise of men, and not the praise of God, if men do but approve and applaud, are not troubled though God does not commend, but condemns them. The praise of men is all the reward they are likely to have. Matthew 6:5: "Verily I say unto you, They have their reward." 'Tis an argument of a carnal heart, and that duties are lost, when distractions are not unwelcome or disliked, but rather the heart is quiet enough with them. If this is the ordinary frame and temper of the heart—to make nothing of heartless performances as long as man cannot see the heart to be absent—it is a sign that hypocrisy reigns. And, alas, hypocrites go to hell through the sanctuary; they tread the broad road, praying, hearing, receiving, all till they fall into eternal condemnation.

Distractions make duties of no effect if they are pleaded for, as if there were nothing of sin or provocation in them. The worse the duties are, many times the performers think them to be the better; they do not eye their own hearts and do not observe their deviations and wanderings; they rest in their mediocre service, as if God should be pleased with the work done and not mind the manner how. We read of some who were bold to expostulate with God because they had fasted, and He took no notice of it. Yet there was good reason for His disliking what they did because, when their voice was heard on high, their hearts were inclined to strife, debate, and wickedness (Isaiah 58:3–4). The scribes and Pharisees contented themselves with an outside righteousness; they did not care that their hearts should be serious and sanctified in their approaches to God. But this righteousness of theirs our Lord pronounces insufficient, and we must go beyond it or we cannot go to heaven.

Distractions make duties of no effect if they come from prevailing and allowed earthly mindedness. How can a devoted servant of mammon, whose heart worships mammon, give acceptable attendance on God? His covetousness, after which his heart goes, proves him to be an idolater (Ephesians 5:5), and his service is most abominable dissimulation. Whatever sin may be beloved, if there is a resolution still to love and hide and spare it, that sin will so distract and draw away the heart from God that no duty that is done can please Him. If we cover our sins, we shall not prosper in our services. If we hide our iniquities in our bosoms because they are dear to us, God will hide His face and refuse to hear us when we cry to Him (Isaiah 59:2).

Distractions make duties of no effect if they hinder all manner of holy and spiritual affections or desires after God. How can the Lord accept a service when the heart is dead and cold as a stone, and altogether senseless and unconcerned that it is so? In such a heart there is no desire to know the Lord and His ways, no inclination to become like Him or to enjoy any fellowship with Him. The apostle said, "Let us have grace whereby we may serve God acceptably" (Hebrews 12:28). Those distractions that altogether hinder the acting and exercise of any grace whatsoever, so that there is no faith, no love, no godly sorrow, no hungering and thirsting after righteousness, certainly must also hinder the success of duties.

Distractions make duties of no effect if, though they are reproved, the person does not strive against them, but allows for sloth, negligence, and formality in attendance upon God. Abundance of idleness was the sin of Sodom; and abundance of idleness is to be found in many a professor, even when engaged in duties of religion. Such bestow no labor upon their hearts; they do not stir themselves up to take hold of God when they call upon His name (Isaiah 64:7). As vinegar to the teeth or smoke to the eyes is very offensive, so is the sluggard to him who sends him. How then must the Lord be displeased with the slothful attendant, and slight his negligent service! Will such service be rewarded? No, no! So far from that, it will be severely punished. He who took no pains to improve his talent is called a wicked and slothful servant in Matthew 25:26. And in verse 30, the sentence is passed upon him: "Cast ye the unprofitable servant into outer darkness: there shall be weeping and gnashing of teeth."

CHAPTER 15

Cautions and Expostulations about Distractions

In applying all that has been said, I shall give the following uses:

I will caution you against the causes of distraction.

I will expostulate with you about these distractions.

I will direct you to remedies against distractions.

I will insist upon several particular duties, and show you how you may with less distraction perform them.

I will speak terror to sinners and hypocrites.

I will conclude with comfort and encouragement to saints who would do better, and who would attend upon the Lord with less distraction.

USE OF CAUTION. If we would be delivered from the effect, we must discover and remove the cause. Health and ease are hoped for in vain while no care is taken to remove the causes of sickness and pain. We shall never be serious in holy duties while we allow and cherish the causes that make our hearts rove and wander from God.

The great causes of distraction that I am to warn you against, and which you are to take heed of, are these:

1. Corrupted nature is the cause of causes; if you trace any sin to its origin, you will see it to be original sin. Corrupted nature never did any duty well, and has no care at all to do anything better. Though the first Adam died several thousand years ago, yet in a sense he lives to this day; he haunts and troubles his whole posterity. And though the old man is crucified with Christ, yet he is not quite dead in any believer while that believer lives upon the face of the earth; and the evil that remains in him will show itself present with him when he would do that which is good. We may truly cry out, "Mystery of iniquity, the great corruption of nature, the mother of wickedness and abominations of the earth." As sin is from hence, so this is the grand obstruction of the serious service of God.

That depravation of human nature which is derived from the first Adam makes the heart of man deceitful above all things, as well as desperately wicked; and for such a heart to act treacherously and to turn aside from God like a deceitful bow in holy duties is indeed but to act like itself. A heart that is totally carnal is so estranged from God that it will never come near Him; you should therefore value the promise of a new heart and a new spirit (Ezekiel 36:26), and beg earnestly that what is promised may be given to you. And though your hearts are indeed renewed, the renovation is but imperfect; there is much of the old nature still remaining, and this, if you are not very vigilant, will catch away your thoughts while you are worshipping the Lord and bring a dampness and coldness upon your hearts.

Original corruption has seized upon all the powers of your souls, and makes all of them averse from attending upon God. The imagination is strongly inclined to wander far off, and the heart and affections are too apt to follow. If a free vent is given to a sinful and vain imagination, the product and offspring of it will be distracting thoughts without number, like the locusts, frogs, and flies that filled the land of Egypt—and with these thoughts religious duties will be corrupted and rendered unacceptable.

Solomon tells us that when man fell from original uprightness, "he sought out many inventions" (Ecclesiastes 7:29); all these inventions were but distractions from God and ways of departing from Him, seeking and trying to find satisfaction and felicity elsewhere, which is indeed to be found in the Lord alone. Let this truth sink deep into you: your hearts do not naturally care for the Lord's service; and if it is engaged in, they are very apt to be careless therein. Cry to heaven so that you may be more renewed in the spirit of your mind, that the old man may be more completely put off and the new man more fully put on. The less your hearts are renewed and sanctified, the more you are likely to be distracted; the more there is of corruption in you, the more it will reveal itself in the duties of religion that you perform.

2. A caution is to be given you against your great adversary, Satan. He catches the Word of God out of the heart; he draws the heart away from the Word and from every other duty. The Spirit of the Lord helps our infirmities and assists us in prayer, but this evil spirit resists us in our supplications. He himself confesses that he walks to and fro in the earth, and goes up and down in it (Job 1:7). His business is to persuade the children of men to do evil, to hinder the doing of good, or to hinder the good that is done from being well done. Who is the man whom this bold enemy will not set upon, since he tempted Christ Himself, who is God and man? If he endeavored to persuade our Lord to worship the devil, no wonder if he persuades us not to worship God, or to be heartless in the worship of Him. Where is the place in which we may be safe and free from his temptations, since he got into Paradise itself and tempted

and prevailed over our first parents there? In secret prayer he is ready to disturb us; he is busy in the sanctuary so that ordinances there may be lost, and that our engaging in them may be for the worse and not for the better. He set upon Judas and entered into him while he was with Christ Himself at the table (John 13:27). We have great reason to watch and pray against this tempter, and to say to him, "The LORD rebuke thee" (Zechariah 3:2).

Can you imagine that when you are about to draw nigh to God, Satan will not draw nigh to you? He will present objects and lay baits for your senses, thereby to divert your minds from the work of God; and not only will he tempt you objectively, but by injection too. Though he cannot look into the heart, yet he can cast a great company of evil thoughts into it; he makes strange impressions upon the fancy, sometimes endeavoring to please it, sometimes to terrify and frighten it, so that in either one way or the other the mind in duties may be distracted. You need to be well aware of this subtle and persistent enemy, and to look to your compassionate High Priest, who intercedes for you with the Father to succor you against the tempter.

When Satan would interrupt you with this and the other trifle, reply to him that you have to do with the great God about business of the greatest and highest consequence, and that it would show both a neglect of God and a slighting of your own souls to be diverted from it. The builders of Jerusalem's walls worked with one hand and held a weapon in the other (Nehemiah 4:17). When you are about the work of God, you should have on the armor of God so that you may stand against the devil's wiles: the shield of faith, the breastplate of love and righteousness, the helmet of hope, and the sword of the Spirit, which is the Word of God. Satan's force is too weak for such weapons as these.

3. A caution also is highly needful against mammon as one of the principal causes of distraction. The service of mammon jostles out the service of God, or so distracts it that it is justly accounted as no service at all. As this world is vain in many other regards, so also in this respect, that sin hinders our service to God from being attained. Instead of being led up unto God by the creatures which He has made, we are drawn away by them from Him; instead of admiring God in the creature, we admire and affect the creature and forget God. The world, being present and visible, takes the senses of men and their fancies; and to walk after the sight of the eye is the way that the heart very well likes (Ecclesiastes 11:9). Hence it is that the invisible God and the things that are unseen, though of eternal excellence and continuance, are totally disregarded, or are but slightly pursued by most men.

How men since the fall have become children in understanding! Mere toys and trifles are of great account with them. Husks are coveted, but that which is indeed bread they have no hunger after. Isaiah 55:2: "Wherefore do ye spend money for that which is not bread? and your labor for that which satisfieth not? hearken diligently unto me, and eat ye that which is good, and let your soul delight itself in fatness." Here it is plainly intimated that diligent hearkening and seriously serving the Lord are hindered by minding things that cannot satisfy. These are things that the flesh longs for, so that its lusts may be fulfilled; these are the things that Satan puts a varnish upon so that they may be the more ensnaring and bewitching. Therefore here lies the great danger lest, while God is near in the mouth, the world fills the heart and steals it from Him.

There are three things in reference to the world that distract thousands of hearts and cause millions of duties to be in vain. The first is love for the world, the second is care about it, and the third is fear concerning it. Of all these you are to beware with the greatest vigilance and concern.

First, take heed of love for the world. If the world has your love, it will have your thoughts at its command, and it will not fail to show its power and to command your thoughts off from God when you attend upon Him. They who are lovers of pleasures more than lovers of God will think of pleasures rather than of God. That rich man in the gospel, while he was alive, had Moses and the prophets as well as his brethren; he was an Israelite in name, called himself a child of Abraham, and professed himself to be a worshipper of the true God. But all his worship was heartless: his heart was intoxicated with sensual delights, his fine purple linen, and the sumptuous fare that every day was provided for him (Luke 16:19). That which the soul takes pleasure in will capture the mind. Sports and pastimes, garbs and ornaments, journeys for diversion and delight, feasts, mirth and music—if the heart is foolishly fond of such sorry things as these, how will they possess the soul, and that in the very house of God when His ordinances are administered! They will be present to the imagination, though really absent, and an imaginary satisfaction will be taken in them; and in the meanwhile the Lord Himself will be forgotten, and communion with Him slighted.

They who are greedy after gain will have their hearts set upon their gain while their bodies are before the Lord. Covetousness commands the thoughts and extinguishes holy desires; while the tongue is speaking heavenly words, the mind will be projecting and contriving how to get the wealth of this world, as if to be rich towards God were but a poor thing in comparison. The earthly heart pleases itself with the thoughts of what it has, and with the hopes of getting more of the world, so that for the flesh more abundant provision may be made. Oh, do not allow the world to have your love and friendship; if you are friends with the world and overly familiar with it, it will have the more easy and ready access into your hearts at any time, and that without the least check. Familiar friends, you know, are bold to come into your home without knocking first.

Second, take heed of care about the world. How these solicitous cares about earthly things distract and divide the mind! When the kingdom of God and His righteousness should be sought, instead we take thought for food and raiment, and things of that inferior nature. Our Lord knew the evil of these cares, and therefore used a great many words to dissuade us from them. He told us that our heavenly Father clothes the lilies of the field and feeds the fowls of the air, which have neither storehouse nor barn; and much more will He provide bread for His children to eat, and raiment wherewith they may be clothed. And they are of little faith who make any doubt of it (Matthew 6:30). If cares about such things prevail, even if duties are done, believers may miscarry in doing their duty; there may be such an anxious solicitousness about this earth and the affairs of it that heaven and the God of heaven may be hardly thought of. Worldly care is one of the things that chokes the Word, and it will choke prayer also; it will hinder the Word from being fruitful, and prayer from being successful. You have leave to cast all your cares upon God who cares for you (1 Peter 5:7). And if, after banishing distrust in God and eagerness after the world, you are careful for nothing in it, you may then by prayer and supplication, with thanksgiving, make your request known unto God (Philippians 4:6). And He will make it known to you that this is the very best course you can take for all manner of supplies.

Third, take heed of fear concerning the world. Our Lord said, "Why are ye so fearful, O ye of little faith?" There is great reason for faith in God, but no reason to fear what the world can do to you. Do not be distracted by fear of worldly losses;

those shall not befall you except as God sees them to be best for you, and they shall turn to your truest gain. Do not be distracted by fear of the world's hatred and the effects of it; the grace and joy of the Holy Ghost can be a hundredfold better even at present than any worldly comfort that man can deprive you of. If an enraged world can keep you from the Lord's service, He will have but little from you. Do not be afraid, therefore, of their terror, neither be troubled, but "sanctify the Lord God in your hearts" (1 Peter 3:14–15). He has promised to be a sanctuary to you. The fear of the lions' den could not scare Daniel from the throne of grace, but he prayed and gave thanks as was usual before his God. If this present world cannot command your love or care, nor raise your fear, you will be mightily fortified against one very great cause of distraction in religious services.

4. Another cause of distraction which I must caution you against is passion and uncharitableness. Passion has a strange and mighty force to transform the whole soul into itself, so that, if this prevails, not only will grace be under a dark eclipse, but even judgment, reason, and common prudence shall seem to be altogether banished. Passion embitters, or rather envenoms, the whole heart of a man, diffusing itself all over so that all is under the power of it. Passion has a monopoly of the thoughts and fixes them upon injuries received; nay, even if they are but imaginary injuries, yet being supposed real, how intently the mind is on them! Perhaps revenge, though so contrary to the nature of Christianity, is wished for and meditated on. Patience indeed possesses the soul, but passion catches the soul away so that it is possessed no longer; all the powers and faculties of the soul are disturbed and are employed in a most disorderly manner.

Passion rises and lies down with the passionate man, and is a very bad companion all the day long; and when duties of religion come to be performed, there is so much anger in the heart against man that God's anger is not feared nor seriously deprecated; neither is His love valued or with any earnestness desired. As the furious man abounds in transgression, so his attendance upon God abounds in distractions; and as these distractions represent the overflowings of wrath, bitterness, and hatred, how displeasing and abominable must they be to the God of love!

Our Lord requires our reconciliation to our brother before we offer our gifts unto God. Matthew 5:24: "Go thy way; first be reconciled to thy brother, and then come and offer thy gift." While you refuse to be reconciled to your brother, how can you expect that God should be reconciled to you? Matthew 6:15: "But if ye forgive not men their trespasses, neither will your Father forgive your trespasses." As charity thinks no evil, so uncharitableness thinks nothing else. It is severe in censuring, forward to judge, not fearing what is threatened, and is itself to be judged (Matthew 7:1–2). It hopes and believes nothing that is good; it bears and endures nothing that it pronounces to be bad, or in the least injurious to it.

Nay, sometimes in prayer, instead of the acting of grace, uncharitableness will be expressed before the Lord Himself. Most unseemly complaints, impious imprecations, and desires are there vented; the divine wrath may fall upon those with whom the passionate are angry. But if they were so severely punished who offered strange fire before the Lord, and fire came forth from the Lord and consumed them, then those who offer this hellish fire of furious and vengeful desires may well fear the vengeance of that fire that is eternal. If you give way to this sinful anger, you give way to the devil; and in this chariot he will furiously drive your hearts away from God in the duties you perform. But the more meek, composed, and sedate your souls are, the more the Holy Ghost will delight to dwell in them, and to vouchsafe His assistance to you.

5. Another cause of distraction is the prevalence of infidelity. Faith is coming to God by Christ Jesus; unbelief is rejecting this Mediator, and the heart's departing from the Lord. Take heed of unbelief, as that which strikes at religion in the very root, and blasts and withers all the fruits of it. Do not doubt the being of God, who gives being to all things that are, and who gave and upholds you in your being to this day. Do not doubt His all-seeing eye, who fills the heaven and earth with His presence. Do not doubt His being ready to be found; all the true seed of Jacob are witnesses for God, that they have sought His face, and that they have not sought Him in vain (Isaiah 45:19). Do not doubt the promises in the Word, which thousands of saints have found accomplished unto their strengthening, supply, and satisfaction. Do not doubt the threatenings that have so often taken hold of them who have boldly ventured upon the sins threatened, so that they have been forced to say, Verily He is a God that judges in the earth, and "like as the Lord of hosts thought to do unto us, according to our ways, and according to our doings, so hath he dealt with us" (Zechariah 1:6).

If unbelief has a place in you, and the great truths of the gospel are questioned or not firmly assented to, how can you be serious in any religious service? How distracted must your thoughts be when you question whether the Lord has any regard what you do or how you do it? This unbelief the great spoiler of your performances, the father of lies, endeavors to promote. He will indeed inject unbelieving thoughts into hearts that have much faith and grace. But as Bernard well says, "Satan only barks when he suggests; he bites when he gains the heart's consent." Oh, never entertain such injections; never give the least consent that they should lodge in you. Look upon them as errant falsehoods that an enemy pesters you with, out of a pernicious design; firmly believe the quite contrary truths so that this belief may influence your spirits and make you more serious when you are before the Lord.

6. The workings of spiritual pride in the heart are another cause of distraction to beware of. It was a good observation of Augustine that other forms of iniquity display themselves in the doing of evil: "Pride lies in wait, as it were, about your good works, to spoil the doing of them, that they may be lost labor." This sin shows itself in several ways, and upon all occasions is apt to stir, puff up, and swell the mind with high and towering thoughts and imaginations. The Pharisee in Luke 18 fasted twice a week, which implies prayer and other exercises of religion. Hereupon he became self-conceited and pride hindered his justification; for he placed his confidence in his own righteousness. What a dangerous distraction is this, when these thoughts are fixed in your heart, that by your prayers and other duties you can make an atonement for your sins, which can indeed be made by the satisfaction and intercession of the Lord Jesus alone!

When the heart is enlarged in prayer, and good expressions come with great fluency from the lips, how apt is he who prays to have high conceits of himself and of his performances! His mind is prone to wander and to think what others think of him, and is sinfully pleased in the imagination that they are mightily pleased and taken with him. Thus pride draws the soul off from God to contemplate its own excellent gifts, and others' admiration of them. Enlargements in holy duties are very encouraging and comfortable when we are humble under them, when we acknowledge the Spirit's grace in them and, though never so much enlarged, despair of acceptance but in Christ alone. But when these enlargements are so treasured that we put them in Christ's place, crediting these blessings to our enlargements when they are actually the fruit of Christ's merit and purchase, here is distracting pride which draws us off from Christ and is very displeasing to the Father. Beware of such thoughts as these: "How well I pray! How broken for sin I appear! How fervent in spirit I seem! What credit and applause I shall get by this performance! What a choice and precious saint I shall be accounted!" Such thoughts are apt to hover about an enlarged heart; but if they are not kept out with an utter detestation of them; the heart will be distracted with hellish pride, however heavenly the expressions of the mouth are.

And as you are to take heed of the workings of pride, so also of every other sin that easily besets you. If, when you are confessing any fleshly or worldly lust, it stirs in you and your hearts have some regard for it and delightful thoughts about it, this will distract your prayer and deafen God's ear. Oh, it is an ill thing to have the heart resolve to spare the sin about which the hypocritical tongue cries aloud so that it may be slain. That sin which your constitutions, callings, or the times in which you live make you most prone to commit, Satan may, in a special manner, endeavor to invigorate so that it may be a great distraction and disturbance to you in your attendance upon God. The grace of God, therefore, should make you most watch against and hate that sin which nature most of all delights in and loves.

7. Another cause of distraction is a zealous affection for an erroneous way. Errors are of several sorts: Some are off from the foundation, others are about the foundation, and a third sort war against and raze the very foundation of religion—

and these last are the most dangerous. The broachers and spreaders of them are called "ravenous wolves who do not spare the flock." Truly the propagators of lesser errors do a great deal of harm, and are called "little foxes." They are so often very prejudicial especially to young converts, and prove a great hindrance to the good work begun in them. Therefore you read in Song of Solomon 2:15: "Take us the foxes, the little foxes, that spoil the vines: for our vines have tender grapes." How errors excite the zeal of the soul! And though they are but about smaller matters, yet they so command the tongue and thoughts that they are more talked of and minded than the great things of law and gospel. Erroneous opinions so possess the heart that the main truths and things of religion are little regarded and even less applied.

When those who are very fond of error are praying, hearing, or engaged in other ordinances, Satan dresses up that error with a disguise of truth, and so presents it to their minds; and their minds are drawn away by the thoughts of it, so that ordinances are ineffectual and lost to them. No wonder that zealots for error are called "wandering stars" in Jude 13; they wander from the way of truth, and this wandering makes them very much to wander from God in holy duties while the eagerness of their spirits is after their mistakes, in which they are so very confident.

Beguiled souls are called unstable in 2 Peter 2:14; the Apostle Paul tells us that they are "tossed to and fro, and carried about with every wind of doctrine" (Ephesians 4:14). The unsettledness of their judgments, and their proneness to run from one error to another, mightily distracts their thoughts; and they are little, if at all, edified by their duties. Errors are very apt to knock at the door when you are attending upon God; and Satan is very busy then to disturb and distract you with thoughts about them. The Lord would be served with greater intention if you did not trouble your heads with doubtful disputations, which you are cautioned against in Romans 14:1, and if you followed that counsel in 2 Peter 3:17: "Beware lest ye also, being led away with the error of the wicked, fall from your own stedfastness."

8. The sloth and laziness of the heart, in refusing to take pains with itself to keep close to God, is another cause of distraction. It is a cause that most commonly prevails, and there is therefore need for caution against it. The work of the heart regarding itself is very hard work indeed. In doing this to purpose lies both the difficulty and the truth of religion. To be wicked and deceitful are the two bad properties of the heart which are natural to it; the wickedness of the heart makes it backward to come to God, while the deceitfulness of the heart makes it very ready to start aside like a deceitful bow and to fly off from Him. Great pains and labor are absolutely necessary to engage the heart to approach the Lord and to abide with Him. These accesses to God are against nature, like rowing a boat against a swift stream or rolling a stone up a steep hill. If the oar is not plied, the stream carries the boat back; leave the stone to itself but for a little while, and how immediately and how far will it run downward! The poet observed the strength of nature's inclination:

> *Use greatest force against nature's will,*
> *Yet it shall recoil upon you still.*

There is need for constant care and industry, and the aid of supernatural grace, or else the heart will never be brought to acquaint itself with God, or to delight in communion with Him.

Take heed of sloth in holy duties and carelessness of spirit, which makes men indifferent and unconcerned what frame their hearts are in, as if in these distractions there were no great sin or harm. The psalmist tells us, "The LORD is in his holy temple, the LORD's throne is in heaven: his eyes behold, his eyelids try, the children of men" (Psalm 11:4), with a pleased countenance. He beholds the upright heart, but He frowns upon all careless servants. Take heed of imagining that there is no need of striving against vain thoughts in the Lord's service. If these are allowed, know that God does not allow them; and if they have place in you, what may they come to at last? The greatest sin ever committed began with a thought, and if the first thought had been utterly banished, the sinful desire would not have been kindled, nor the deed done.

I have spoken of the causes of distraction. With great heed you are all to beware of them; for if you give way to these, they will corrupt all your duties. I read in the old law that nothing that had a blemish was to be offered to God in sacrifice; this shows that Christ, the great Sacrifice, was without blemish and without spot, and it intimates what our duties ought to be. But if distractions and their causes are not taken heed of, your services will be no better than a sacrifice would have been if it had all the forbidden blemishes spoken of in Leviticus 22:22: "Blind, or broken, or maimed, or having a wen [warts], or scurvy, or scabbed." Such a sacrifice must have been very hateful if it had been offered to the Lord.

USE OF EXPOSTULATION. I shall expostulate the matter with you about these distractions in your religious perfomances.

Without distraction you can mind your secular affairs; and why should you not be more intent and serious about your eternal concerns? What is a small dot compared to the whole circle of the heavens? What is time, which ends almost as soon as it begins, to eternity that will never end at all? Temporal afflictions are light, and burdens are only for a moment. Temporal felicity is but a pleasant and short dream, and is chased away as a night vision. But eternal woes and joys are woes and joys indeed; they are perfectly possessed all at once, altogether. As for the woes, there can be no hope of any release; as for the joys, there is no room for any fear of deprivation.

Without distraction you can hear or read news or a pleasant story; and is not a religious duty of far greater importance to you? Shall the pleasing of the fancy be minded more than the securing of the soul? Shall the state of affairs in this world be asked about, and will you not seriously inquire into your own spiritual state, and mind what is likely to become of you when you go into the other world where you will be fixed in blessedness or misery, both of which will be unalterable?

Without distraction heretofore you have hearkened to the evil one, and with great studiousness have contrived to commit sin; and if the worst master was thus attended upon, shall not now the best be regarded much more? Have you not devised wickedness, and set yourselves in an evil way (Psalm 36:4)? And will you not now with as great thoughtfulness devise how to do good, and with an undistracted purpose set upon doing it? The apostle would not only have you change your master and, being free from sin, become servants of righteousness (Romans 6:18); but as you formerly served sin, so you should now serve righteousness. Be as forward, serious, and diligent in holy duties as ever you were in the works of darkness.

Without distraction you have thought upon injuries and have meditated on revenge; and shall not reconciliation with God and your own salvation be minded with greater intention? You think much of the wrongs that others do to you; think more of the injury you have done to God's justice, and how you have sinned against your own soul in provoking His wrath against you. Jeremiah 7:19: "Do they provoke me to anger? saith the Lord: do they not provoke themselves to the confusion of their own faces?" Let the thoughts of the many talents you owe swallow up the thoughts of the few pence which are owed to you.

How often, and for how long a time together, has mere vanity commanded your thoughts and hearts? And will you not watch with your Lord, and be in His work for an hour? Proud imaginations and silly suppositions of your having that wisdom, wealth, excellence, and esteem that you do not actually have have prevailed, and you have set yourselves on high in your own fancies. How fixed have divers sorts of wickednesses been in your speculations! And why should not your spirits be much more fixed upon God and your duty toward Him?

Food, raiment, and providing for your families are minded in good earnest, and without distraction; and should you not seek the kingdom of God and His righteousness with far greater heedfulness? Why should there be so much distraction in minding the one thing needful? If you do not mind the good part quickly, you may miss it eternally; it may soon be too late to seek it. But if now you choose it, your hearts being seriously set upon it, you shall have it, and that good part shall never be taken away from you (Luke 10:42).

CHAPTER 16

Directions to Remedies against Distractions

USE OF DIRECTION. I am to direct you to proper remedies against distraction in religious performances. The disease, I grant, is difficult to cure, but the Great Physician can heal any distemper with ease. Having therefore your eye and dependence upon Him, use these following remedies:

1. Let your first thoughts every morning always be good ones. A heart well seasoned with such thoughts in the beginning of the day is likely to be in the better frame in holy duties, and better inclined all the day long. As soon as you are awake, let your souls work heavenward and be lifted up to the God who is there. Such souls He is pleased with, and delights to communicate His grace to. If the Lord has the first fruits of your hearts, the first thoughts and desires, you are likely to be blessed with better thoughts and desires afterwards. In old times, the first-fruits being offered to God, His blessing was upon the whole harvest. And though you take pains with your hearts in the morning, remember, at no time of the day may you let down your watch and become utterly regardless of your own spirits; for if you are, corruption will quickly return, though it has had never so great a check, and that with great force and violence. Thus, when the sea fled and the Jordan

was driven back, within a little while they both returned to their former course and channel.

"When I awake," said the psalmist, "I am still with thee" (Psalm 139:18). He saw himself under God's special care and compassed with His favor as with a shield; and God's thoughts about him, so full of tender mercy and lovingkindness, and amounting to so vast a sum, were very precious and delightful to think of. And whenever he awoke, how his heart worked towards the Lord in a way of gratitude and love! Begin the day well, and all the day long keep your hearts with all keeping. If you would not have your thoughts vain in duty, let them not be allowed to be vain at any time. In the space of time between your solemn duties, be frequent in holy ejaculations and mental applications unto God; this will mightily help to keep a sense of Him upon your hearts, and the more undistracted your service will be when at your set times every day you attend upon Him.

2. Be sensible that the preparation of the heart in man is from the Lord (Proverbs 16:1). Look unto Him, therefore, to prepare your hearts for every duty you engage in. Cries for preparation should be the first cries, and then cries afterwards are likely to be to a better purpose. Preparation for duty goes before profit by it; and when the Lord vouchsafes to prepare, He intends to bestow benefits. His preparation causes prayer to be so seriously and fervently made that it shall in no way meet with a denial. Psalm 10:17: "Thou wilt prepare their heart, thou wilt cause thine ear to hear." In this preparation, the Spirit of the Lord affords a mighty help. There is a liberty and freedom in the duty that is to be performed; and the more free the heart is to the duty, the more free and enlarged it is likely to be in the duty. Clogs and weights are removed; and among these clogs, distraction and deadness may well be reckoned.

The heart prepared by the Spirit and grace of Christ is disentangled from the world and stands aloof from it so that it may draw nearer to God. It is made to see how worthy sin is of its most bitter sorrow and utter detestation. With a holy indignation it says, "What have I to do any more with any of my iniquities?" The prepared heart prizes the blessings it is about to petition for, and longs to appear before God, from whom alone they can be obtained. It is delivered from the vain and injudicious spirit of this world, and by the Spirit which is of God knows the worth of those things that are so freely given by God. This preparedness of heart, then, must be a great preservative against distraction.

3. Pray for the fulfilling of that promise wherein the Lord has engaged to give you a heart to know Him. They who are ignorant of God must be ignorant also how to attend upon Him. If their knowledge is only notional, and they do not know Him as they ought, they will not attend on Him as they ought. Lay hold therefore upon that good word of promise in Jeremiah 24:7: "And I will give them an heart to know me, that I am the LORD: and they shall be my people, and I will be their God: for they shall return unto me with their whole heart." And Hebrews 8:11: "For all shall know me, from the least to the greatest." This knowledge of God will have a mighty influence upon your hearts to bring your very thoughts into captivity and obedience. We read in 1 Samuel 2:3 that "the LORD is a God of knowledge, and by him actions are weighed." And they who rightly know this will take care to serve Him in sincerity.

True knowledge of God will bring a great awe of Him upon your spirits. His majesty, glory, and holiness will strike you into great humility and reverence. How you will be emptied of yourselves, and your souls and thoughts swallowed up in God, when He causes His excellence to pass before you! The appearance of the Lord so obscures and darkens all other things that they are counted as not worth minding. Therefore the prophet says in Isaiah 24:23, "Then the moon shall be confounded, and the sun ashamed, when the LORD of hosts shall reign in mount Zion, and in Jerusalem, and before his ancients gloriously." The eye of this God whom you attend upon is jealous, and yet it is all-seeing. Oh, take heed of being deceived, as if God would be mocked by man, and man not be the worse nor smart for it. Galatians 6:7: "Be not deceived; God is not mocked: for whatsoever a man soweth, that shall he also reap." If your duties are only like a sowing of mere chaff, how can you expect to reap any good by them? The good angels themselves reverence the Lord whom you are worshipping; the apostate ones tremble before Him. The better you know Him, the more godly your fear will be; and fear will unite your hearts and thoughts both to God and to the work and duty He requires.

4. **Be very careful to cherish the grace of hope in your hearts, and look upon holy duties as highly valuable privileges.** The greater your expectation is of the truest benefit and advantage, the more intent and fixed will your thoughts be. The apostle prayed to the God of hope for the believing Romans, that they might abound in hope by the power of the Holy Ghost (Romans 15:13). Hope has an earnest expectation, and the better the things are that are hoped for, the more earnest the expectation is. The word the apostle used for "expectation" is an emphatic word, and signifies "to look for a thing with the head lifted up, and with great intention of both eye and mind." What a remedy such a hope would be against distraction! When hope is very low, the mind runs very much upon matters of discouragement and is deadened by it. And the best things of all being almost despaired of, the heart is more apt to wander after things that cannot profit. But hope is compared to an

anchor in Hebrews 6:19: "Which hope we have as an anchor of the soul, both sure and stedfast." It keeps the souls steady and fixed upon what is hoped for until it is enjoyed.

Duties are not only to be engaged in as being due to God, but we are to be persuaded that giving what is due to God is the way to receive still more and more from Him. In these duties, our hopes should be high in Him who is most high; we are not able to conceive how much He can do for us. We are to hope in Him as a most liberal and all-sufficient Giver; we are to expect His deepest compassion in our distresses and afflictions, and especially when we are weary and heavy laden with the burden of our iniquities. We are to expect the unlocking of the unsearchable riches of Christ, which are enough to enrich the whole beggared progeny of Adam. And all who come to Him shall certainly experience the riches and fullness of that grace that dwells in Him. The plowman plows in hope, and hope fixes his thoughts upon the precious fruits of the earth, which in harvest he expects to reap. Oh, study the promises of God, which are exceedingly broad; they are wider than the earth and sea, and they reach as high as the highest heaven. Hope for the promised blessings of all sorts— temporal, spiritual, and eternal—and, the more strong and lively hope is, the more it will fix your mind, revive your spirits, and quicken your desires.

5. Another remedy against distraction is a fervent love. As love is the first and great command, so it is a most commanding affection. Love is the weight that sets all the wheels going, and inclines them in the same way that love itself is inclined. Some have said that the soul of man is where it loves—on the object beloved—rather than in the body, the tabernacle where it dwells. The reason is because love so commands the mind and thoughts after it. If your love is set upon God, love

will set your thoughts upon Him. How intent are the thoughts of the covetous upon their beloved gain! The pleasures that the voluptuous dote on are hardly ever out of their mind! If love for God constrains you to attend upon God, it will bring your thoughts along with it, and will very much restrain them from wandering.

The love of God can never be produced by corrupt nature, nor by the mere force of reason; it is a special grace of the Lord's Spirit, and to Him you must make application for it. Christ died that He might bring you to God, and love is the soul's going to Him. In the name of Christ, lift up your earnest petitions that this grace of love may be wrought in you in truth; and, being wrought, that it may continually be increased. The Lord said that He will write His laws on your hearts. Oh, pray that this great command to love Him may be written in deep and lasting characters; and if the Lord once becomes your desire and delight, the duties you perform will become more pleasant, delightful, and undistracted. God is light, and in Him there is no darkness, nothing but what is desirable. All excellencies in the creatures are derived from Him, and the streams are but little if we look to the Fountain from whence they all come. This God, as excellent and glorious as He is, is willing in Christ to be yours. Such loveliness! Such lovingkindness! What love do these call for from you! Let nothing be able to draw away your love, and the less will your thoughts be drawn away from Him.

6. *Be very poor in spirit.* A pressing sense of your spiritual necessities will make you very intent and serious in begging supplies from above, for from thence alone can you be supplied. They who are pinched with poverty think much of how poor they are! They have such a smart feeling of their needs that they can scarcely think of anything besides. When the con-

demned malefactor on the cross cried for a pardon, surely the apprehension of his danger made his words and his thoughts go together. When a man who is famished asks for bread, no doubt his mind is very much upon that bread which may prevent his starving. Be sensible how great the needs of your souls are, and that only the Father of spirits can give you the mercy and grace that you need; and the more sense you have of these, the less distracted you will be in your applications to Him.

Our Lord pronounced the poor in spirit "blessed" (Matthew 5:3). Their petitions come from an inward sense of their want, and of the worth of blessings; and, being earnest petitioners, they shall be successful ones. You who feel your guilt, and who fear divine wrath, must think of a pardon, and the desirableness of it, when you ask for it. You who are sensible of your maladies, how intent will your minds be upon the Lord, the healer of His people! And you will have little wish to think of something else when you are begging to be cured! True poverty of spirit will constrain you to an undistracted seeking of that gold tried in the fire to enrich you, and that white raiment to cover you (Revelation 3:18), without which you must be wretched and miserable because you will be poor and naked.

7. Let conscience be very tender, vigilant, and faithful. Such a conscience will be very helpful to prevent distraction, or to quickly put an end to it. It will observe and fetch home the truant and straying thoughts, and bring them to your duties. Conscience (and I distinguish between a tender conscience and a scrupulous one; a scrupulous conscience is a great cause of distraction; for scruples are most apt to ruin and pester the mind during holy duties) acts in God's name, by His authority, and urges obedience to His laws. If it is truly enlightened and faithful, it will insist upon the right manner of obeying. Conscience takes strict notice of the whole soul

and all its actings; and this officer of God especially does this in the soul's approaches to the Lord. A sense of being under God's eye makes the faithful conscience's eye more strict and ready to spy all faults so that they may presently be amended. In holy duties, such a conscience will be very busy; it will earnestly protest against vain and distracting thoughts and will say, "What? Make such thoughts here, when God and His work only are to be minded?" Such a conscience will not patiently tolerate the presence of evil when good is contemplated; cannot brook with patience; it stirs up the lusts of the Spirit against those of the flesh so that the law of the mind may prevail more against the law in the members (Romans 7:23).

If conscience is asleep in your performances, how sorry and sinful will they be! The heart will be dead, the thoughts will wander far away, and no holy affections will be stirring. Pray hard for a good conscience, a conscience not only purged by the blood of Christ from all the guilt which by dead works you have contracted, but also by the same blood healed of its sleepiness, stupidity, and all its other faults.

Such a conscience may more effectually check your hearts from roving and trifling in attendance upon God. Look before you with the eye of strong and steady faith, and see as far as death and judgment, and into eternity, and then judge whether, for your carelessly performed duties, your Lord will say, "Well done, true and faithful servants!" The apostle, having looked as far as his own, and also the world's last day, wherein the heaven shall pass away with a great noise, the elements melt with fervent heat, and the earth and the works therein shall be burned up, rationally infers that Christians' conversations should be very well ordered, and duties of godliness most undistractedly and seriously performed. "Seeing then that all these things shall be dissolved, what manner of persons ought ye to be in all holy conversation and godliness?" (2 Peter 3:10–11).

8. Another remedy against distraction is growing in grace, and in the knowledge of Christ (2 Peter 3:18). This will keep you from being led away by error, and will make you more steadfast in duty as well as truth. When grace shall be perfected in glory, distraction will be perfectly cured; and here on earth the cure is advanced as grace is augmented. The more grace you have, the higher value you will set upon communion with God; and this will fill your hearts with holy zeal and indignation against everything that may divert your minds and be an obstruction to this communion. The more grace you have, the more you are filled with the Spirit; and when you pray in the Holy Ghost, your prayer will be "fervent prayer" (James 5:16). How much of the heart and soul will be therein! And the same Spirit, in hearing and in other ordinances, will keep your hearts with God when they are about to turn to the right hand or to the left. The more grace you have, the more your treasure will be in heaven; and you are told in Matthew 6:21 that "where your treasure is, there will your heart be also."

Now, that there may be an increase of grace, Christ must be better known; for 'tis from Him that the first grace is derived, and all additional degrees of it. Study Him more and understand His fullness, who "fills all in all" (Ephesians 1:23). Desire with the apostle that you may "know him, and the power of his resurrection, and the fellowship of his sufferings, being made conformable unto his death" (Philippians 3:10). If you conform to the death of Christ and are crucified and dead to the world, and the world to you, the things of the world will appear without form and comeliness, and will be less able to distract your minds and ensnare your affections. And if you feel the power of Christ's resurrection, your hearts and thoughts will rise with Him; and at what a cost will you seek those things that are above! The angels, when here on earth, are doing what God commands them, and so they are still in heaven, as to their thoughts and as to the happiness they enjoy. You should be heavenly when about your earthly business, but especially when you are attending upon the God of heaven. And the more experientially you understand Christ to be risen, the less will things on earth be minded, and the higher will your hearts rise and ascend after Him.

9. Ever commit the keeping of your souls to God Himself in well-doing (1 Peter 4:19). Apprehending how liable you are to distraction in His service, entreat that He would undertake for you. He who spans the heavens, and holds the winds in His hand so that they stir not in the least against His will, certainly is able to keep your hearts undistracted in your duties, and close to Himself. The Lord makes and searches, and newly makes and fixes the heart of man; and none of this is to be done by any power less than His. When David's soul followed hard after God, he acknowledged that it was the Lord's own right hand that upheld him (Psalm 63:8). Call in help from heaven against distraction if you would be helped effectually. The Christian, not only when he is leaving the world but when he is engaging in any religious duty, should say with the psalmist in Psalm 31:5, "Into thine hand I commit my spirit." He and He alone can keep it in a serious and composed frame.

CHAPTER 17

Advice for Avoiding Distractions in Religious Duties

USE OF ADVICE. This use shall be of counsel as to some particular duties on which I shall insist, showing you how they may be performed with less distraction. I shall speak of four duties: reading the Holy Scriptures, hearing the Word preached, prayer, and communing at the Lord's Table.

DUTY 1. Read the Holy Scriptures, and so that you may read with less distraction, be firmly persuaded of the Scripture's divine authority and verity. When you look into the Bible, remember that it is a book of God's own making you have in your hands. The writers of it were but His penmen; they did not their own mind and will, but God's mind and will, and were moved and inspired by the Holy Ghost. To be distracted and careless of what you read is to condemn God by disregarding His Word. Mind what you read, for the Scriptures can make you "wise unto salvation" (2 Timothy 3:15). You may securely trust His Word; its light is infallible, it is certain in its promises and threatenings, and it will by all be found true to eternity. "The word of the Lord endureth forever" (1 Peter 1:25).

Believe the Scriptures' perfection and sufficiency as a most full and plain means to guide you to everlasting blessedness. Here you are faithfully warned to flee from the wrath to come, and from sin which deserves it; and here you may find God's counsel, by which you may be guided safely to glory. You need not be distracted and doubtful in your own minds, as if in the Scriptures God's mind was declared only in part. Man's additions are needless, nay, impious. Proverbs 30:6: "Add thou not unto his words, lest he reprove thee, and thou be found a liar." And men's traditions are vain. Heed the Word of God as that which enlightens the eyes, converts the soul, and rejoices the heart; as that which is "profitable for doctrine, for reproof, for correction, for instruction in righteousness: that the man of God may be perfect, thoroughly furnished unto all good works" (2 Timothy 3:16–17).

Look upon the Scriptures as directed to you in particular, and laying an obligation upon you, as if they had dropped from God out of heaven into your hand. The Word forbids sin in you as well as in any one else in the world; its commands reach you as truly as if you had heard the Lord calling to you by name to yield obedience. The offers of the gospel are really made to you and, upon acceptance, the blessings offered are your own; if they are refused, how can you escape the wrath of Him who speaks to you from heaven for your good (Hebrews 12:25)? This particular application is also made by Solomon, whose calls the Word a "goad" and a "nail fastened" to stir you up to your duty, and to settle you in it. Proverbs 22:19–20: "That thy trust may be in the LORD, I have made known to thee this day, even to thee. Have not I written to thee excellent things in counsels and knowledge?"

See the Lord Himself as being near by you when you read His Word, and hear Him bidding you take heed how you read. As He has magnified His Word above all His name, so He requires a special regard for it. He looks with approbation and pleasure upon that man who trembles at His Word (Isaiah 66:2), but when He perceives instruction to be hated, and that

His law is cast behind the back, He admonishes such forgetters of God to consider what this neglect will cost them if not repented of, and He threatens to tear them in pieces, so as that there shall be none to deliver (Psalm 50:17, 22).

Lift up your eyes to heaven for instruction from the Spirit, by whose inspiration the Scripture was given. 'Tis the Spirit of Christ who opens men's understandings to understand the Scriptures (Luke 24:45). Be humbly sensible of your ignorance and proneness to error and mistake. A promise is made to the humble and meek that God will guide them in judgment, so that they shall judge aright of things, and He will teach them His way (Psalm 25:9). Cry to the Lord to make you mind what you read, and to profit by what you mind. Desire Scripture knowledge so that what you know may have a deep impression upon your spirits, may excite holy and gracious affections and resolutions in your hearts, and be mightily effectual unto a more thorough amending of your ways and doings.

In all your ways seek light from the Holy Scriptures so that every step you take may be rightly ordered. Do not go in any way that the Word of truth calls a false way. How well and wisely does he walk who can say with the psalmist, "Thy word is a lamp unto my feet, and a light unto my path" (Psalm 119:105). When you go, let this Word lead you, and then when you sleep there is a promise to keep you; and when you awake it will talk with you, and will tell you what you must avoid, believe, and do, so that you may be blessed forever. "The commandment is a lamp; and the law is light; and reproofs of instruction are the way of life" (Proverbs 6:22–23).

And as the Word talks to you, so you should talk of the Word you read; it will fix it in your thoughts and hearts the better, and will make your discourse more edifying to others. Deuteronomy 6:6–7: "And these words, which I command thee this day, shall be in thine heart: and thou shalt teach them diligently unto thy children, and shalt talk of them when thou sittest in thine house, and when thou walkest by the way, and when thou liest down, and when thou risest up." The more the Word is written in your hearts, the more grace is there; and the more you speak of it to others, the more it will administer grace to the hearers.

DUTY 2. Hear the Word preached. And that you may hear the Word with less distraction:

Look beyond preachers unto the God who sends them and speaks to you by them. Look beyond the earthen vessels unto the treasure they bring; and look upon the Word that is preached as "the glorious gospel of Christ, who is the image of God" (2 Corinthians 4:4, 7). Preachers of the gospel are Christ's ambassadors; they are sent to treat with you about peace with God, and by them God beseeches you to be reconciled (2 Corinthians 5:20). How beautiful should you count the feet of them who preach the gospel of peace and bring glad tidings of good things! Such tidings are too good to be heard distractedly and heedlessly. And He who sends them is too great to be thus condemned. When you sit before the ministers of Christ, the stewards of the mysteries of God, remember what our Lord Himself said in Luke 10:16: "He that heareth you heareth me; and he that despiseth you despiseth me; and he that despiseth me despiseth him that sent me."

Apprehend who are ready, if you hear distractedly and without care, to catch the Word away from you as soon as it is spoken. Evil angels are compared to the fowls of the air, who hover about the sower to devour the seed as soon as it is sown (Luke 8:5). These evil spirits are fitly compared to fowls, for they are many; and how they come flocking into our religious assemblies! It is desirable to have souls come flying to Christ, as doves to their windows; but it may startle us to understand that devils come flocking into churches to catch away the Word that is preached there! These enemies are as many, and are like fowls above us; and consequently it is not so easy to resist them. How many sermons have these evil angels stolen! And the sermons they have stolen, they will have them to show against heedless hearers at the day of reckoning.

Make a covenant with your eyes so that your hearing may be the less distracted and more attentive. Do not fix your sight upon any alluring and ensnaring objects, or on anything that may divert you. And as your eyes must be turned away from beholding vanity, that you may be quickened in the way of your duty, so be sure to keep your eyes waking. If sleep locks up the senses, how fast must the heart in the meantime be barred against the Word of God! Eutychus, a church sleeper, is an example on record. He sank down with sleep while Paul was preaching, fell down, and was taken up dead (Acts 20:9). They who sleep during a sermon scandalously reject and despise the Word preached. Satan is a most wakeful witness against them, and his arms are the cradle in which they are rocked.

Beg that the Lord Himself would open your hearts to attend to His Word. It was He who opened the heart of Lydia, and then she attended to those things which were spoken by Paul (Acts 16:14). It is the Lord who makes way for the Word into the mind so that it may be heeded and understood; and He makes way for the Word into the heart so that the heart may be changed and cleansed thereby. John 15:3: "Now are ye clean through the word which I have spoken unto you." It is dreadful to provoke the Lord, so as to be like provoking Israel, to whom Moses spoke in Deuteronomy 29:4, "The LORD hath not given you an heart to perceive, and eyes to see, and ears to hear, unto this day." And it will be worse if you love to have it thus. Oh, think thus, that distracted hearing may cause the Word of life to become deadly to you, and God may judicially and yet justly harden your hearts lest you should see, hear, understand, and convert and be healed (Isaiah 6:10).

Let the Word preached be mixed with faith and received with love. The apostle tells us that the Word preached did not profit the hearers of it, "not being mixed with faith in them that heard it" (Hebrews 4:2). Commands will be heeded and obeyed that are indeed believed to be of God. Threatenings and promises that are most firmly credited cannot but be minded and have a mighty influence. The Word also is to be received in the love of it so that you may be saved. The design of this Word is your deliverance from sin and misery, your peace, your purity and perfection, your eternal redemption and glory; and therefore it commends itself exceedingly to your affections. A sincere love for the Word will command the thoughts of the heart and hinder the Word from being disregarded.

Remember that the Word that you hear is your life. There is a carelessness of life in heedlessness and distraction in hearing the Word of God. Deuteronomy 32:46–47: "Set your hearts unto all the words which I testify among you this day,…for it is not a vain thing for you; because it is your life." Proverbs 7:2: "Keep my commandments, and live; and my law as the apple of thine eye." Isaiah 55:3: "Incline your ear, and come unto me: hear, and your soul shall live; and I will make an everlasting covenant with you, even the sure mercies of David."

And further, to fix your attention on the Word preached, be persuaded that you who are now in the sanctuary must shortly stand at the judgment seat of Christ, and the Word which He has spoken, the same shall judge you at the last day (John 12:48). Then you must render an account of your stewardship, and how all your talents have been improved; and you must be judged, and receive according to your works. And I am sure that the sentence that will then be pronounced, whether it is of absolution ("Come, ye blessed") or of condemnation ("Go, ye cursed"), will be heard without distraction. Both the one and the other of these sentences must be heeded by all upon whom they are passed—the one being so very comfortable, and the other so terrible and confounding.

DUTY 3. A third duty that I shall insist on is prayer. So that you may with less distraction call upon the name of God:

Consider whose name you are taking into your mouths. Deuteronomy 28:58: "this glorious and fearful name, THE LORD THY GOD." It is a name that should never be on the lips without the profoundest reverence in the heart. "The gods that have not made the heavens and the earth, even they shall perish from the earth, and from under these heavens" (Jeremiah 10:11). But "the LORD is the true God, he is the living God, and an everlasting king: at his wrath the earth shall tremble, and the nations shall not be able to abide his indignation" (verse 10). This God to whom you pray is infinitely more above you than the greatest emperor is above the meanest worms that crawl upon the ground. How should you look to the frame of your spirits when you are before Him! The passion of fear calls the blood in to the heart so that the vitals may be fortified; and truly the grace of fear will call in the thoughts of the heart so that duties performed to so great a Majesty may not be a heedless trifling with Him.

Sequester yourselves from other businesses to attend on prayer; the more you are disentangled from your secular affairs, the more free and fit your hearts will be to be poured out before the Lord in your supplications. The further you step out and off from the world when you come to knock at heaven's gates, the more certainly the door will be opened to you. If mammon has your thoughts and desires when you are praying to God, you have a jealousy-provoking idol in your hearts while in His presence; and how offensive must this be to Him, to see an idol where He chooses to dwell! "One thing," said the psalmist, "have I desired of the LORD, that will I seek after" (Psalm 27:4). Other things were esteemed worthless by comparison. Let not other matters distract you when you are calling upon God so that you may pray in prayer, and do nothing else but pray. Remember, distracted confessions increase guilt and wrath; distracted petitions ask for a denial, and distracted praises will tend very much to stop the current of mercies.

Be persuaded that the Lord will attentively mind what you pray if you intently mind what you pray for yourselves. He takes pleasure in uprightness, and this Heart-searcher well knows who is sincere. Not so much as a sigh or groan from a sincere soul shall be disregarded. If you cry from your heart for mercy, mercy shall compass you about (Psalm 32:10). The prophet tells us that the Lord "hearkened and heard" (Jeremiah 8:6). Indeed, most do not speak aright; they do not repent of their wickedness, saying, "What have we done?" But those who speak aright, and are truly sensible of the evil of their doings, fervently pray to have their sins covered, and all their defilements purged away, the Lord who hearkens so attentively will surely hear all such cries, and will in no way deny what is cried for. Believe in the mighty efficacy of fervent prayer, what rich returns this trading to heaven brings in, and what treasures prayer is a key to unlock, that you may be enriched thereby! A sacred coveting of these unsearchable riches will make you mind what you are doing when you are praying to partake of them. The apostle tells you, for your encouragement, "There is no difference between the Jew and the Greek: for the same Lord over all is rich unto all that call upon him" (Romans 10:12).

Cry earnestly for the Holy Spirit of promise. You will never pray aright, or to any purpose, without His aid. The Holy Ghost is called the Spirit of grace because all true grace is from Him, and so are all gracious desires and actings. He is also called the Spirit of supplication; all acceptable confessions, petitions, and thanksgivings are of His indicting. This Spirit is promised; and how ready is our heavenly Father to give the Spirit to any who ask Him! We read that "He that searcheth the hearts knoweth what is the mind of the Spirit, because he maketh intercession for the saints according to the will of God" (Romans 8:27). Saints' prayers are called "the mind of the Spirit." He makes them to be according to the will of God—and that not only as to the matter of them, but also as to the manner. The Spirit of God at first moved upon the face of the waters, and how many useful creatures did He produce out of a chaos of confusion! And if that Spirit moves upon your hearts in prayer, He can keep your thoughts so that they do not stir away from God. He can cause faith, godly sorrow, hope, humility, and love to be in actual exercise; and the more grace is exercised, the less distracted and more successful prayer will be.

Let vigilance and watching go before; keep pace with prayer, and follow after it. Why does a Christian have new eyes and light but that he might watch with the one and by the other? Our Lord joined watching and praying together. Prayer without watching will be heartless; watching without prayer will be insufficient for your security. Watching with prayer makes it more serious, and to succeed the better. The apostle said, "The end of all things is at hand: be ye therefore sober, and watch unto prayer" (1 Peter 4:7). Watching unto prayer summons the whole soul with all its faculties to attend upon God, and to prepare to meet Him. We also read in Colossians 4:2: "Continue in prayer, and watch in the same with thanksgiving." Watching in prayer is a mighty help against the heart's straggling. This straggling is the sooner observed, and the straggling thoughts to be presently reduced. And he who watches after prayer diligently and with all thankfulness observes the answers of prayer. And thus, to do so will strongly induce you to give yourselves more to prayer in good earnest, and to wrestle with Him with whom you so often prevail.

DUTY 4. Commune at the Lord's Table. And that this may be done with less distraction:

Let there be more serious self-examination before you engage in that holy ordinance. First Corinthians 11:28: "But let a man examine himself, and so let him eat of that bread, and drink of that cup." Look into the state of your souls, and your state is good if you know the true God so as to love Him and prefer Him in your choice before all other things, and if you know Christ so as to rely upon Him, with consent to be ruled by Him as your Lord and Savior. John 17:3: "This is life eternal, that they might know thee the only true God, and Jesus Christ, whom thou hast sent."

Take great notice also of the present frame of your hearts, that you may know in what graces they are weakest, what kind of lustings of the flesh are most apt to prevail, and what things are most likely to distract your minds and draw your hearts away when you are at the Table. Your watch hereupon will be the stricter, and your thoughts will run the more upon the particular graces that are to be strengthened, and upon the sins too that are to be struck dead by the power of the death and crucifixion of Christ Jesus. Remember that Christ Himself is really present at His Table; and His eye, which is as a flame of fire, observes the frame of every heart. Fix your eye upon your own hearts since Christ's eye is upon them.

Let the death of Christ put you in mind of what you were, and would have been still, if He had not died for you. You would have been dead under the law, under the damning sentence of it; and you would have been dead in trespasses, dead to God and to anything that is truly good, employed in nothing but dead works, and thereby fitted to destruction. And how should your thoughts be seized by the obligation your Lord has laid you under in freeing you from death and eternal destruction by laying down His own life as a ransom for you!

When the apostle said that he determined not to know anything save Jesus Christ and Him crucified (1 Corinthians 2:2), it showed upon whom his thoughts were fixed. Our thoughts at the Lord's Table should be fastened to Christ as He was to the cross. We should behold, admire, and be suitably affected when we behold Him who is equal with God, in the form of a servant, in the likeness of sinful flesh, and humbling Himself so low as to become "obedient to death, even the death of the cross" (Philippians 2:8). Let the worth of the Person suffering, the merit of the sufferings themselves, and the value of the benefits thereby procured be believed—and how can we heedlessly think on such things?

Take due notice that, when Christ was dying, He gave the charge to His disciples that they should engage in this ordinance as a memorial of Him. Christ's death was infinitely more than if all creatures that have life had lost their lives to make an atonement. Just when He was ready to make His soul an offering for sin, He bade us to do this in remembrance of Him. First Corinthians 11:23–24: "The Lord Jesus the same night in which he was betrayed took bread: and when he had given thanks, he brake it, and said, Take, eat: this is my body, which is broken for you: this do in remembrance of me." The command of such a Lord, that Lord dying, and dying such a meritorious death, and in that death expressing love which surpasses knowledge; and the command given so that He might still be and live in our remembrance—this, if well weighed, will make us mind what we are doing and will prevent distraction.

The sacramental elements and actions, with their significance being understood, will be a great means to fix the thoughts of the communicants. When your eyes behold the bread, let your faith behold the body of Christ. When you see the bread broken, believe that Christ was wounded and bruised for your iniquities, and bore them in His body on the tree. When the bread is given to you, understand what a gift of God Christ is. When you take the bread into your hands, let your hearts be open more fully to receive Christ Himself, and to receive still more from Him. And when you eat the bread, be sure to feed upon Christ, the Bread of Life, by faith. Rely upon His crucifixion as your reconciliation, for we are "reconciled to God by the death of his Son" (Romans 5:10). And as bread is the staff of life, so let this Bread of Life be your soul's stay; rest upon Christ for spiritual life and strength more and more abundantly to be given you.

When you perceive the wine given apart from the bread, think to yourselves that your Lord's life was indeed, though not against His will, taken from Him; body and soul were separated, though neither from the Godhead. Look beyond the wine to the blood of Jesus; believe it to be more precious than gold that perishes, and that, being the blood of Him who is God, it can do away the greatest guilt and the foulest spots and stains of the sins of men. When you drink the wine, believe the cup of blessing to be indeed the communion of the blood of Christ (1 Corinthians 10:16). Rest on this blood to justify you from all things for which the law condemns you. Rest on this blood to pacify your consciences and heal the wounds that sin has made there, to purify and heal all the plagues of your hearts, to make you perfect in every good work, and to open a way for you into the holiest of all—not only to procure constant access to the throne of grace, but an abundant entrance into the everlasting kingdom. Thus you will be helped against distraction in this ordinance, if the heart understands and applies what is visible to the eye.

Advice for Avoiding Distractions in Religious Duties

That you may be the more serious in this ordinance of the Lord's Supper, remember that therein you solemnly renew covenant with the God of heaven, you give yourselves over to Him, disclaim all other lords and owners, and profess to take Him to be your Lord, your God, your Guide, your All. Oh, mind what you do that you may be sincere in doing it. God has no pleasure in fools (Ecclesiastes 5:4), who do not consider with whom they have to do; who do not consider what evil they do when they do that which is good in a distracted and deceitful manner.

In this ordinance, the broad seal of heaven is put into your hand to confirm your faith in the new covenant, and so that you may with greater confidence expect the accomplishment of its promises. He who rests on Christ, and who hungers and thirsts after righteousness, may rejoice in this ordinance more than a bankrupt person would do who receives the release of all his debts, and with it a will and testament sealed whereby a plentiful estate is made over and assured to him. Communicants solemnly profess a recommitment; they tie themselves faster and more strictly to the Lord. There is nothing you have or are but is His. Will and heart and thoughts are to be ever in His service, and at His command.

Be sensible how dreadful the guilt is that is contracted when you are guilty of the body and blood of the Lord; and this guilt comes upon you by distracted, careless, and unworthy receiving. First Corinthians 11:27: "Wherefore whosoever shall eat this bread, and drink this cup of the Lord, unworthily, shall be guilty of the body and blood of the Lord." The communicant whose heart does not care how distracted it is, how he condemns the Son of God, His blood, and His benefits! If he does not count them worth seriously thinking of, surely he does not think them worth his thankful acceptance. How precious is the blood of Jesus! And what a heavy load is the guilt of such blood! It is sad not to be saved by the blood of Christ; but much sorer under the guilt of it to sink lower into damnation. Temporal punishments that are inflicted upon receiving amiss may be terrible; but how much worse are eternal judgments! Oh, give your hearts into God's hand so that He may keep and order them at the table and afterwards; the more there is of His help in the performance, the less will there be of distraction, and of your own infirmities.

CHAPTER 18

Terrors of Distractions and Encouragements to Believers

USE OF TERROR. There is terror unto sinners and hypocrites, upon all whose attendance upon God is devoid of care and full of allowed distraction. They freely grant their hearts a liberty, and their naughty hearts take it, to be whatever they please, and to run off to whatsoever they have a mind for, as if the Heart-searcher's eye had neither sight nor jealousy.

The duties of such whose hearts thus run away from God are not steps toward heaven, but toward hell. If they hear the Word of God, they do not understand it; the gospel is hidden from them, and the god of this world blinds them (2 Corinthians 4:3–4). If they attain to some kind of knowledge of the truth, they hold it in unrighteousness. Sin grows stronger by their very duties; its power is not at all impaired by them for, thinking by their duties to make some amends for their sins, they are more emboldened to commit iniquity. When they have done their heartless services, God is more angry with them. Thus the Jews of old, choosing their own ways, and their souls delighting in their abominations, having no delight in God or in His ways, the hatefulness of their sacrifices is thus expressed in Isaiah 66:3: "He that killeth an ox is as if he slew a man; he that sacrificeth a lamb, as if he cut off a dog's neck; he that offereth an oblation as if he offered swine's blood; he that burneth incense, as if he blessed an idol." Not only by impenitence and hardness of heart, but by heartless duties, the performers of them treasure up unto themselves wrath against the day of wrath.

When terrible calamities force sinners to cry with some earnestness for relief, their cries may be altogether in vain. God may justly be as heedless of them in their distress as they were impiously heedless of Him in their devotions. Thus He threatens, when "distress and anguish cometh upon you, then shall they call upon me, but I will not answer; they shall seek me early, but they shall not find me." Nay, which is worse, He says, "I will laugh at your calamity; I will mock when your fear cometh" (Proverbs 1:26–28). They deserve to be mocked in their misery, whose duties were a mocking of God to His very face. The prophet speaks to the same purpose in Zechariah 7:13: "Therefore it is come to pass, that as he cried, and they would not hear; so they cried, and I would not hear, saith the LORD of hosts."

And if He is deaf many times to sinners' cries on earth and will afford them no help, certainly in hell He will be utterly regardless of their miseries. No prayers are heard, no petitions are granted, that come from that place of woe (Luke 16:24–27).

When sinners and hypocrites are in hell, what bitter reflections will they have upon their distractions and negligence in the service of God here on earth! How terribly will conscience reproach and lash them, because in their day "they knew not the things that concerned their peace"! Most wretched and self-destroyed fools, conscience will call them, because it was no more in their thoughts to fear and escape eternal vengeance—because they were so eager after things on earth, which now can be enjoyed no more, as to neglect the everlasting bliss and glory of the heavenly kingdom! They who will not do their duty to God now without distraction shall be forced without distraction to think of their misery to eternity. The greatness of their woe will immovably fix their thoughts upon it. A sinner in outer darkness shall thus reflect upon himself, and his unconceivably deplorable and desperate case: "Oh, what flames, what terrors and agonies do I suffer! What poisoned arrows of the Almighty are within me! How glorious is His power in my destruction! How righteous, though intolerable, is His indignation! And what I suffer, I must suffer without any hope at all of any ease or end." The undistracted thinking of all this cannot but make hell to be hellish beyond measure. Knowing now the terrors of the Lord, let all be persuaded to take heed of trifling with a holy and jealous God, and of doing His work negligently, who will so severely punish all evil, slothful, and unprofitable servants.

USE OF ENCOURAGEMENT. Let this be of encouragement and comfort to believers, who would fain do more and better than they do, and with less distraction serve the Lord. They should indeed go with a low sail because of their leaky hearts, which are so weighed down and hindered by indwelling sin, when they are attending upon God; and yet, that they may not be quite cast down, let their eye be upon these grounds of consolation.

1. Let the saints know that it is from that grace which is within them that their distractions are burdensome to them. As it is by the softness of the heart that the remaining hardness of it is felt, so it is by grace in the heart that its wanderings are perceived, and, being perceived, become a matter of concern. The apostle speaks by way of encouragement in 1 Corinthians 10:13: "There hath no temptation taken you but such as is common to man." So I say, the distraction that is your burden

is so far from proving that you have no grace that it is common to all gracious souls, while militant in this world; and it is part of their militancy to be conflicting with distracted thoughts. And the stronger they grow in this conflict, the more successful they are. God has renewed the will so that it consents that the law of God is good; it desires more undistractedly and with delight to do whatever is required; only the remaining flesh is otherwise inclined. The apostle's reflection upon himself and what he did was not altogether without comfort. Romans 7:25: "I thank God through Jesus Christ our Lord. So then with the mind I myself serve the law of God; but with the flesh the law of sin."

2. God will not impute those distractions to believers which they desire so truly and earnestly to be freed from. It is a good rule that they are not imputed if they are violently brought into the heart, and if their stay and abode there is not allowed. The man who labors under the palsy, his head and his hands shake against his will; he does not shake either of them himself, but wishes both were more steady. The saints' distractions are against their wills; they do not willingly distract themselves. The Lord does not call them hypocrites for these, and they misspeak if they call themselves by that name simply because their hearts sometimes start away from duty against their will and purpose. What saint on earth could stand if God should mark such iniquities and miscarriages as these (Psalm 130:3)?

3. Christ's satisfaction and intercession may comfort believers under their distractions and all their infirmities. Our Lord, by suffering death, has made complete satisfaction for their iniquities and for the sins of their holy duties. God is so well pleased in the Son of His love that very faulty and imperfect duties being presented by Christ are well taken. Oh, what a difference is there between a duty as it comes from us and as

it has its defects covered with Christ's righteousness, and is so presented to the Father! The apostle tells us of the glory of the grace of God, "wherein he hath made us accepted in the beloved" (Ephesians 1:6). When Christ was upon earth, the satisfaction He made was sufficient to make reconciliation for all sins and defects. And now that He is in heaven, He does not cease to intercede for believers; a thousand faults may be found in their best duties, but how absolutely faultless and prevailing is this intercession of their Advocate!

4. In many of those duties that doubting saints have thought to be nothing but sin and distraction, God sees and owns the actings of grace. He sees some fire in the smoking flax which He will not quench, though there is much that is offensive with it. He sees some greenness in the bruised reed, though there is much that is dead, and yet He will not break it (Matthew 12:20). His eyelids try the children of men, and He has a gracious regard for the acts of grace and faith, though they are but as a grain of mustard seed. Christ Jesus is said to be quick of understanding in the fear of the Lord (Isaiah 11:3). He knows what key will open every heart, and when He will open, none can keep shut. He can bring the most fearless and foolish to the fear of God. And where the fear of God is in truth, though it is a lower degree, He easily discerns it. When a well of water is muddy at the top, there is purer water working up from the spring at the bottom. When the heart is very much discomposed and distracted in duty, if under all these infirmities there is a working and stirring of the grace of God, He will both observe and be well pleased with it. He will not utterly reject a duty when there is a hearty desire to do it well and a hearty grief that it is done no better.

5. The Lord is ready to give a blessing to those means that He Himself has appointed for the cure of these distractions. These means are effectual when the Spirit makes them so. And "is the spirit of the LORD straitened?" (Micah 2:7). What infirmity is too great for Him to help? What heart is too roving and unruly for Him to settle? The means must be used, so cry for help that you may be helped to cry; hear the Word with a desire to feel its power, that you may hear it to better purpose. Take encouragement from the mighty Spirit who is so ready to accompany God's institutions. He can fit you for your duty, fix your hearts in it, and crown the doing of it with the blessings that are promised. And when your hearts are fixed, it is a reason why your mouths should sing and give praise.

6. When militant saints come to be triumphant, their distractions, and their complaints because of them, will be at a perpetual end. In heaven they shall be out of Satan's reach; he shall resist them no more. They will have left this world, which so often troubled both their heads and their hearts, and will have exchanged it for a world that is infinitely better. Their perfected spirits will be perfect in their operations; nothing of imperfection will cleave to what the glorified saints above are doing. The vision of God, face to face, will fix the mind and thoughts upon Him eternally. Having once looked on Him, they will never care to look off again. Perfection of holiness, love, delight, and joy must forever hinder even the least wandering. None can in the least be weary of the work that is done in heaven, for it is so full of pleasure. Revelation 4:8: "They rest not day and night, saying Holy, holy, holy, Lord God Almighty, which was, and is, and is to come." And completely glad may they well be, that such a pleasant employment must never come to an end.

If all this congregation, with their pastor, can but get safely into the house not made with hands, eternal in the heavens, oh, what thoughts and apprehensions shall we have! How shall we be filled with joy and wonder at what we shall then behold! Having entered and being swallowed up in the joy of our Lord, shall we not then cry out, "Ah! What a difference there is between this heavenly country and the most desirable earthly inheritance! The sun is but a small spark compared to that light which we now see. When we look upward, we admire the heavens outside, the firmament with all its shining luminaries; but now we plainly see that heaven is much more glorious within. What an excellent society is this innumerable company of angels that we are among! How every glorified saint and member of Christ resembles his Head, being all fair and with no spot remaining! How pleasant is the harmony where there is no sin, no sorrow, no defect, or discord! These hallelujahs which we now join in, how ravishing and transporting are they, not like the distracted services which we used to perform together in the sanctuary! We are all now fixed in this glorious place, and shall never go out again. Our complaints are quite ended, and never again shall we do the least amiss. We are indeed without fault before the throne of God, and we shall live and reign, triumph and magnify the Lord forever!"

Thus have I finished my discourse concerning distraction in attending upon God, a fault whereof all are guilty; most make nothing or very light of it, and very few mind to have it mended. My design herein has been to do some service to the church of Christ, that their worship may be more pure and spiritual, being freed from those wandering thoughts that distract and defile it; and that the best of Lords may still have better and more acceptable service from all of you, and from myself also. While we are in this world, truly this world is too much in us; it is suitable to our senses, and apt to entice and draw away our hearts. Let the eye of faith pierce through the clouds and see heaven's joy and glory, and then this world's vanity will be the more apparent. How vain it is for you to be so thoughtful about it and eager after this world. When faith has seen how God is attended upon by saints and angels above, it may help to kindle in you a holy zeal and a vehement desire to more resemble those excellent attendants, and to serve the Lord more gladly and seriously here below.

Oh, cry out to have the cure of distractions carried on further toward completeness. Live as strangers and sojourners here on earth, not concerned about worldly things as others are. Declare plainly that you are born from above, and let your hearts and thoughts more and more ascend there. Carry yourselves as fellow citizens with the saints, and as those who are of the household of God. Let there be more of God, and more of grace in all you do and speak, in all the powers of your souls, in all the duties you perform. And think with gladness and longing of that blessed inheritance, when you shall be fully delivered from sin and death, and from all deadness and distraction in mind and heart. Everlasting rest must eternally exclude whatever now troubles you. How perfectly healed and perfect in holiness and joy will you be in every way when you have attained to the glorious liberty of the sons of God!